Cover photograph: This photo
presents some often neglected
foods in children's daily diets.

Book Three   **Health and Growth**

Julius B. Richmond, M.D.
Elenore T. Pounds, M.A.
Irma B. Fricke, R.N., M.S.

In consultation with
Orvis A. Harrelson, M.D., M.P.H.
Norman H. Olsen, D.D.S.
Wallace Ann Wesley, Hs.D.

Designed by Norman Perman
Anatomical Art by Lou Barlow, AMI

Scott, Foresman and Company

Authors

Julius B. Richmond, M.D. Professor
of Child Psychiatry and Human
Development, Harvard University;
Director, Judge Baker Guidance
Center; Chief of Psychiatric Service,
Children's Hospital, Medical Center;
Professor and Chairman, Department
of Social and Preventive Medicine,
Harvard Medical School.

Elenore T. Pounds, M.A. Writer;
lecturer; former Directing Editor,
Health and Personal Development
Program; classroom teacher; author
of *Drugs and Your Safety* and other
Health and Growth Enrichment Booklets.

Irma B. Fricke, R.N., M.S. Former
Director of School Nursing, Evanston
Public Schools, District 65, Evanston,
Illinois; recipient of the 1971
William A. Howe Award in school health.

Consultants

Orvis A. Harrelson, M.D., M.P.H.
Director of Health Services, Tacoma
Public Schools, Tacoma, Washington.

Norman H. Olsen, D.D.S. Chairman
of the Department of Pedodontics and
Dean of the Dental School, Northwestern
University, Chicago, Illinois.

Wallace Ann Wesley, Hs.D. Director,
Department of Health Education,
American Medical Association, Chicago,
Illinois.

ISBN: 0-673-04322-3

Advisors

Robert W. Benoit. Principal and teacher,
Bessie C. Rowell School, Franklin, New Hampshire.

Thea Flaum, B.A. Former editor, *Safety Education,*
National Safety Council, Chicago, Illinois.

Willie D. Ford, Ph.D. Professor, Nutrition
and Home Economics, Grambling College,
Grambling, Louisiana.

Gladys Gardner Jenkins, M.A. Lecturer in
Education and Home Economics, University
of Iowa, Iowa City, Iowa; former member
National Advisory Council on Child Growth
and Human Development; author of *Helping
Children Reach Their Potential;* coauthor
of *These Are Your Children.*

Ruth Leverton, Ph.D. Science Advisor,
Agricultural Research Service, United States
Department of Agriculture, Washington, D.C.

Maria Elena Sanchez, M.A. Primary teacher,
Hayward School District, Hayward, California.

Dieter H. Sussdorf, Ph.D. Associate Professor
of Microbiology and Immunology, Cornell
University Medical College, New York,
New York; coauthor of *Methods in Immunology.*

Joan S. Tillotson, Ph.D. Consultant in
Movement Education; former teacher at
elementary through college levels.

Health Editorial Staff

Thelma H. Erickson, Executive Editor; Terse
Stamos, Directing Editor; Jean Carr,
Associate Editor; Patricia Siegert and
Rosemary Peters, Assistant Editors.

Designer

Norman Perman, B.F.A. Graphic Designer,
Chicago; Guest Lecturer, University of
Illinois, Circle Campus, Chicago, Illinois;
past President, Society of Typographic Arts.

Regional offices of Scott, Foresman and Company
are located in Dallas, Texas; Glenview, Illinois;
Oakland, New Jersey; Palo Alto, California; Tucker,
Georgia; and Brighton, England.

Contents

1 What Do You Know About Your Body?

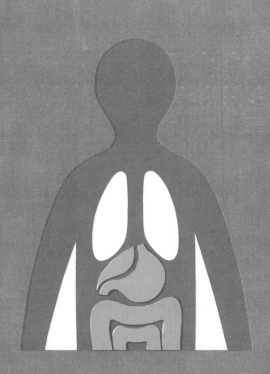

How Do You Look Inside?

You know that the skin is your body's cover and that inside you is a framework of bones called the *skeleton.*

But do you know about other parts inside you that you cannot see?

What part of you works like a pump?

Where is your voice box?

What part of you stores dissolved sugar from the food you eat?

What part helps the body use this sugar?

You can find the answers to questions like these on pages 9 to 26. You will learn many other things about your body on these pages, too, as you pretend you are visiting a Health Museum. At this museum there is an exhibit called the Transparent Talking Woman. She is made of plastic and is wired for sound so that she can "talk." As she talks, she tells how she looks inside.

If you could go to the real museum, you would find that lights turn on inside the parts of the body she is telling about. Perhaps you can imagine that the lights are turning on as you read what she would say to you.

The script on pages 9 through 25 has been adapted and is used by permission of The Hinsdale Health Museum, Hinsdale, Illinois.

What Does the Transparent Woman Say?

Hello there, boys and girls. I am going to tell you a story—a wonderful story about how you look inside, where usually you can't see at all.

If you will do everything I ask you to do, we will have some fun.

Are you ready?

Put your hands on the sides of your head. Do you feel some hard bone? Your brain is inside that bone. The bone helps keep the brain safe.

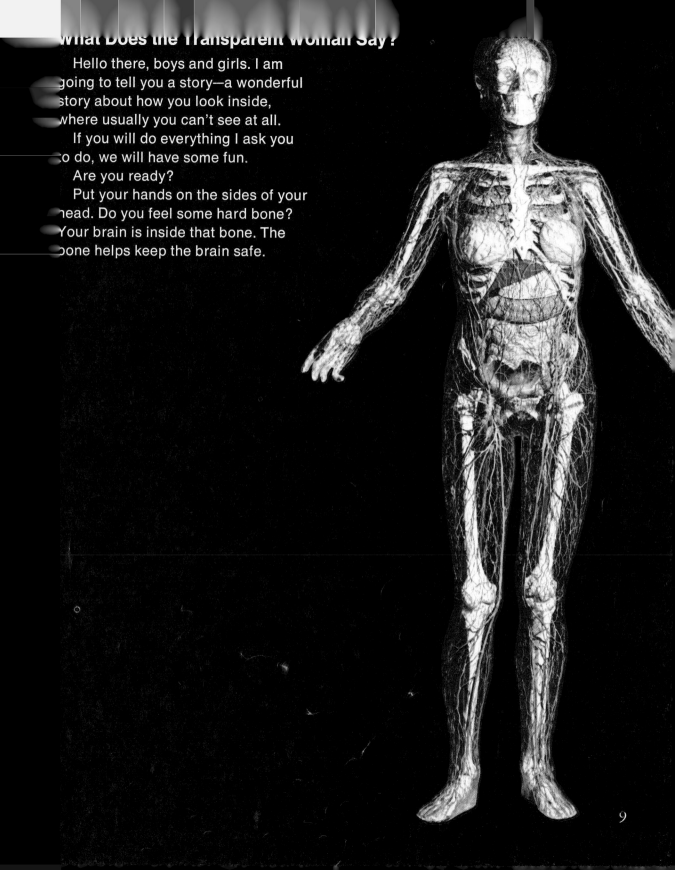

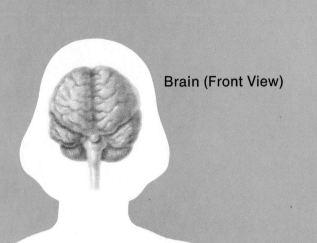

Brain (Front View)

This is the brain.

The brain is the place where you think. How does the brain get things to think about? Before I tell you, I want you to do several things.

First, blink your eyes. Now pinch your ears—but don't pinch too hard. Put out your tongue. Sniff with your nose. Wiggle your fingers and rub the skin on your arm.

It is the eyes, ears, tongue, nose, fingers, and skin that give your brain things to think about. The eyes send sight messages to the brain. The ears send sound messages to the brain. The nose sends messages of smell. The tongue sends messages of taste— whether things are sweet or sour, for example. The fingers and skin send messages about the feel of things—whether they are hot or cold, rough or smooth, round or square. All these messages are sent to the brain over *nerves*. And this is the way the brain gets things to think about.

The brain sends orders for action, too. It sends orders for chewing food that is eaten. It sends orders for running and jumping and playing.

The brain sends orders for clapping the hands. All right, everybody, clap! There! The brain sent orders for clapping the hands.

The brain sends orders for every move that you choose to make.

You know how sleepy you feel at night. That is because the brain, as well as the rest of the body, slows down from the day's activity. So you go to sleep. But some of your organs —such as your heart and lungs—go on working all night long. The part of the brain that tells *them* what to do never stops working.

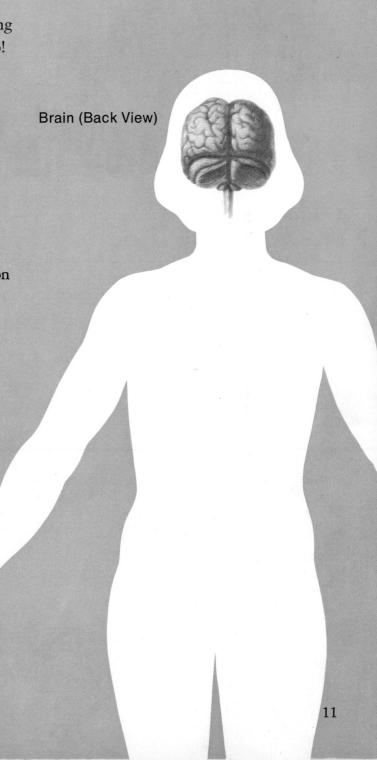

Brain (Back View)

11

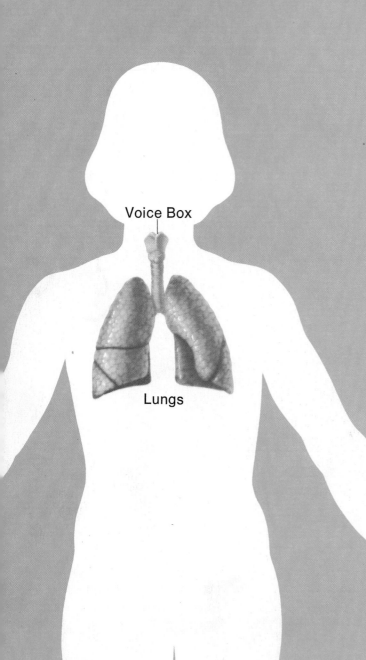

Voice Box

Lungs

Near the top of the throat is the voice box.

Its real name is the *larynx.* Say a big long "A-a-ah." There! You said it with the larynx. There are cordlike parts inside the larynx which move—this makes the sound when you talk. Sometimes when you have a cold, your larynx swells up, and you are hoarse. You have *laryngitis!*

Here you see the lungs.

They are as light as balloons because they always have air in them. Now breathe in and out slowly. Can you tell that air is going in and out of the lungs?

Next close your mouth tightly. Hold your nose shut. Stay this way as long as you can. Hold it . . . HOLD IT. There! If you were playing fair, you couldn't hold it any longer, could you? Do you know why? A part of the air, called oxygen, is so important that you must have it all the time. You can't see it, but it is there—and you need it to keep you alive.

This is the heart.

You can put your hand on your chest and feel your heart beating. Only it really is not beating at all. It is *pumping*. For the heart is a pump. It pumps the blood through little tubes called *blood vessels.*

No matter where you might cut yourself, blood will always come out—for blood is in these little tubes everywhere inside you all the time.

The blood carries food and oxygen through the blood vessels to all parts of the body. The body needs the food and oxygen to stay alive and to grow.

The blood picks up oxygen in the lungs. Later you will learn how food gets into the blood after it has been broken down and changed into liquid form, or *digested*.

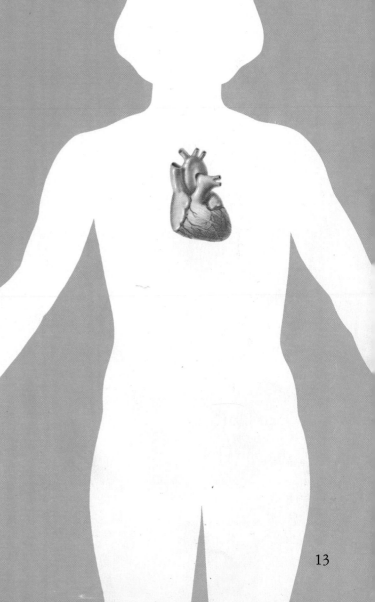

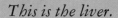

This is the liver.

It is a very large and very busy gland. One thing it does is to make a juice called *bile.* You will learn more about bile very soon.

Another of the very important things the liver does is to store the dissolved sugar from foods you eat. When blood flows through the liver, it picks up just enough sugar to give you energy to do the things you usually do—things like walking and combing your hair. When you do something that calls for extra energy—something like swimming or running a race—the blood picks up the extra amounts it needs of this stored sugar.

Liver (Front View)

—Gall Bladder

On the underside of the liver is the gall bladder.

Another name for the *bile* made by the liver is *gall*. It helps digest the fat in the food you eat. Here you can see the sac that stores the gall, or bile. This sac is called the *gall bladder*.

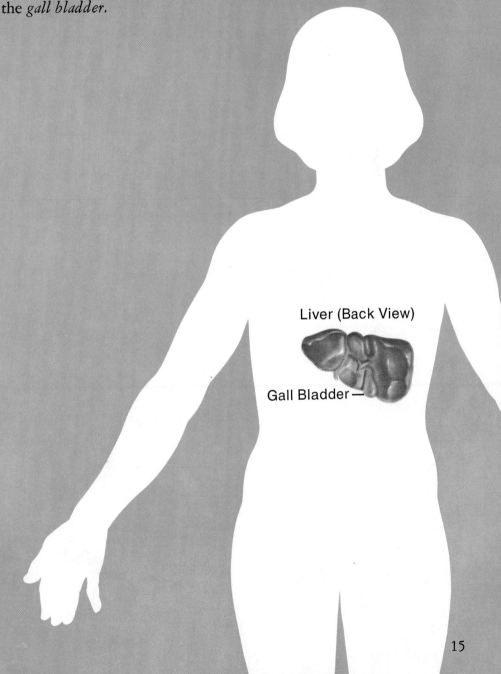

Liver (Back View)

Gall Bladder —

This gland is the pancreas.

The pancreas makes some useful juices to help you digest the food you eat. Groups of cells within the pancreas also help the body use sugar.

Now I am going to tell you more about how food is digested.

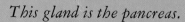

Here is the stomach.

You know what happens when you drop a lump of sugar in water, don't you? It dissolves. Food has to be dissolved before it can get into the blood to be carried to all parts of the body.

It is not easy to dissolve things like apples and steak and nuts and lots of other things you eat. It can't be done just with water. But it can be done by means of special juices.

Food starts to digest when you are chewing it and mixing it with the juice called *saliva.* Saliva is in your mouth. This saliva begins to change the food so it can be digested.

After you swallow the food, it goes right on being digested. It is churned around and is mixed with other juices that are in your stomach.

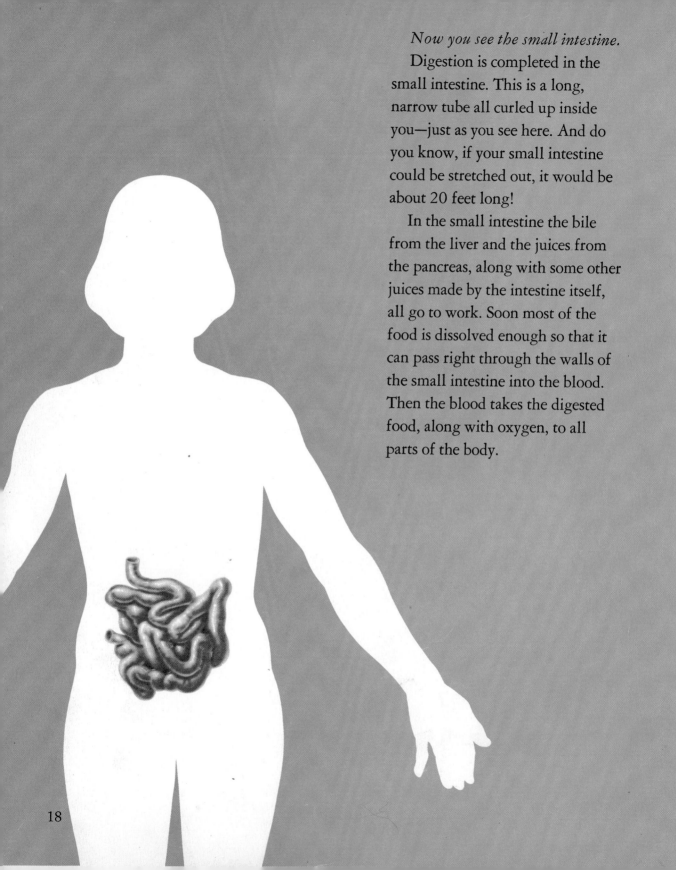

Now you see the small intestine.
Digestion is completed in the small intestine. This is a long, narrow tube all curled up inside you—just as you see here. And do you know, if your small intestine could be stretched out, it would be about 20 feet long!

In the small intestine the bile from the liver and the juices from the pancreas, along with some other juices made by the intestine itself, all go to work. Soon most of the food is dissolved enough so that it can pass right through the walls of the small intestine into the blood. Then the blood takes the digested food, along with oxygen, to all parts of the body.

The rest of the food, the part that did not dissolve, goes into the large intestine. This is a big tube. Here the excess water is removed. The waste food is slowly pushed along into the *rectum.* The rectum is the place where the waste food stays until it leaves the body in a bowel movement.

If you want to have good digestion, you can help by chewing your food until it's easy to swallow. This will give your stomach and your intestines a chance to do their work.

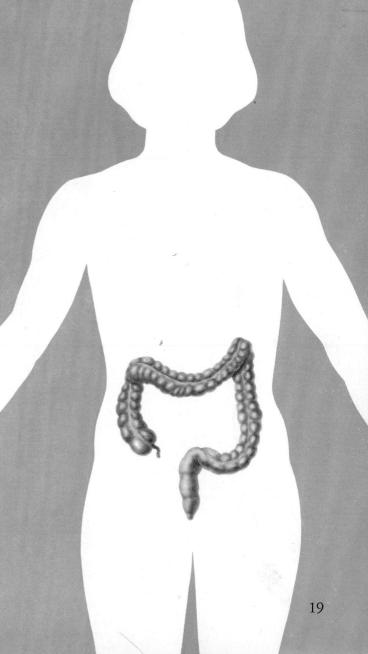

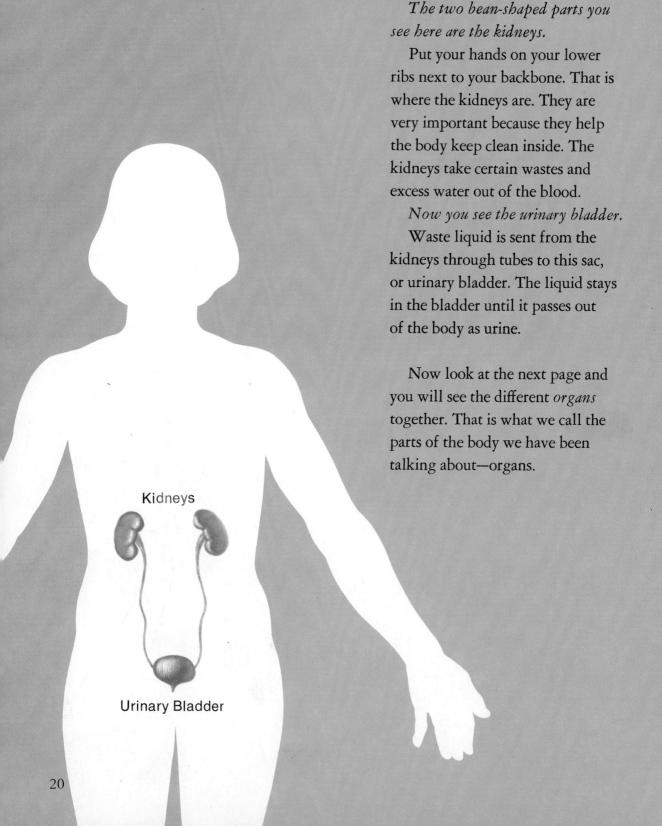

The two bean-shaped parts you see here are the kidneys.

Put your hands on your lower ribs next to your backbone. That is where the kidneys are. They are very important because they help the body keep clean inside. The kidneys take certain wastes and excess water out of the blood.

Now you see the urinary bladder. Waste liquid is sent from the kidneys through tubes to this sac, or urinary bladder. The liquid stays in the bladder until it passes out of the body as urine.

Now look at the next page and you will see the different *organs* together. That is what we call the parts of the body we have been talking about—organs.

Kidneys

Urinary Bladder

You have now read about some of the exciting things that happen inside people. And you can better understand how the organs in the body work together to help you grow and keep alive and stay healthy.

You can help your body do its work. You can eat enough of the right kinds of foods and drink lots of milk. Also try to exercise every day and get plenty of fresh air. Another thing you should do is go to bed *on time*. Then you will get the sleep and rest you need.

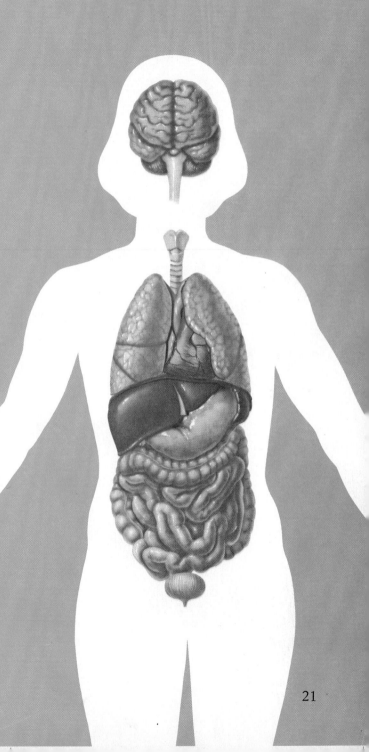

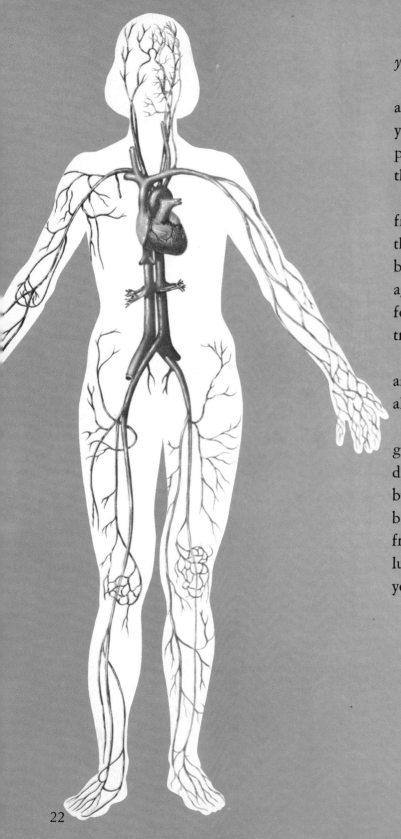

There are blood vessels all over your body.

Blood vessels are in your hands and feet, in your eyes and ears, in your stomach, in your brain, in all parts of your body. There are thousands of miles of them.

These blood vessels carry blood from the heart to the lungs, back to the heart, out to every part of the body, and then back to the heart again. It takes less than a minute for the blood to make this round trip.

The blood carries digested food and a fresh supply of oxygen to all parts of the body.

The blood also carries a waste gas called *carbon dioxide.* Carbon dioxide is made when sugar is burned for energy inside you. The blood carries this carbon dioxide from all parts of your body to your lungs. Then when you breathe out, you get rid of carbon dioxide.

These are the nerves.

Maybe you wonder how messages of hearing, seeing, smelling, tasting, and touching get to the brain. These messages travel *to* the brain over *sensory nerves,* or nerves from sense organs like the eyes and ears. The messages travel over these nerves the way your words travel along telephone wires when you talk to a friend.

Messages travel *from* the brain over *motor nerves* to the muscles. These messages are orders telling the muscles when and how to move.

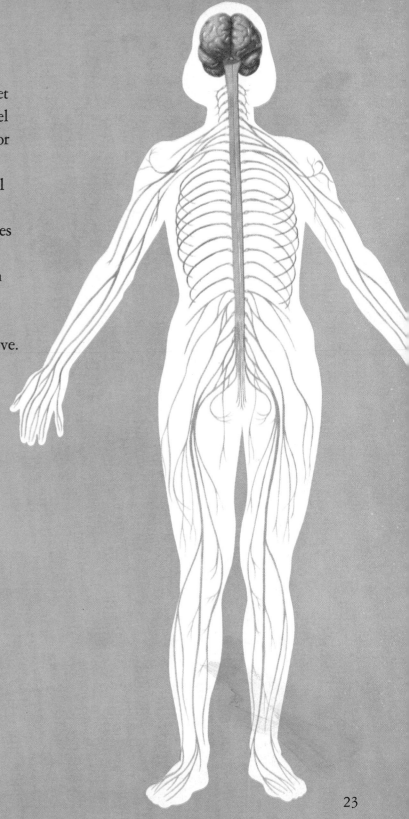

23

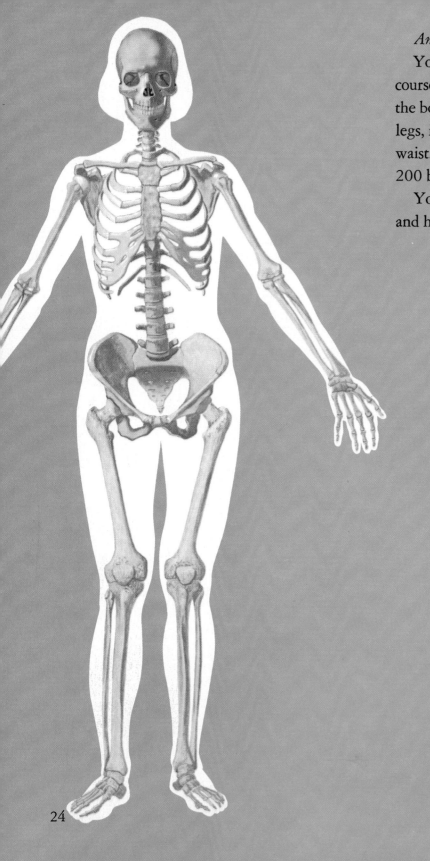

And here are the bones.

You cannot see your bones, of course. But you can feel them. Feel the bones in your head, in your legs, in your arms, and at your waist. Altogether, you have some 200 bones in your body.

Your bones help hold you up and help you move about.

Now suppose you wave your arm. Do you know why you can wave it? It is because you have *muscles,* as well as bones. You can feel the muscles in your arm, can't you?

The muscles were all left out of the Transparent Talking Woman so you could see inside the body. But your muscles are there all right. You'll just have to imagine you can see them. They are fastened to the bones and they pull the bones to make you move.

Lift your arm high. The shoulder muscles are pulling up the bones of your arm.

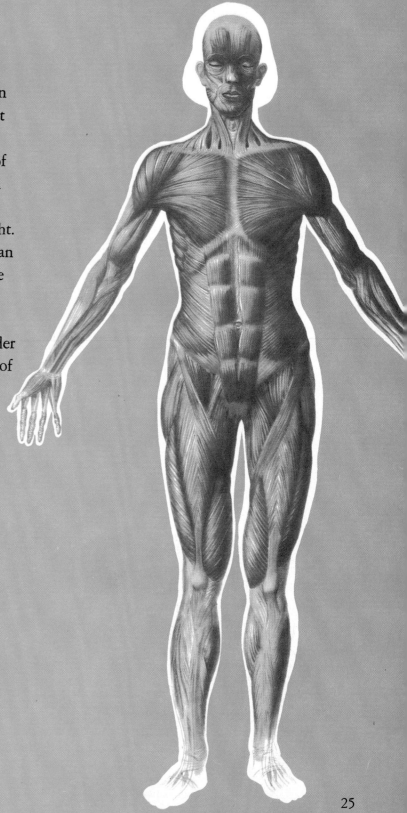

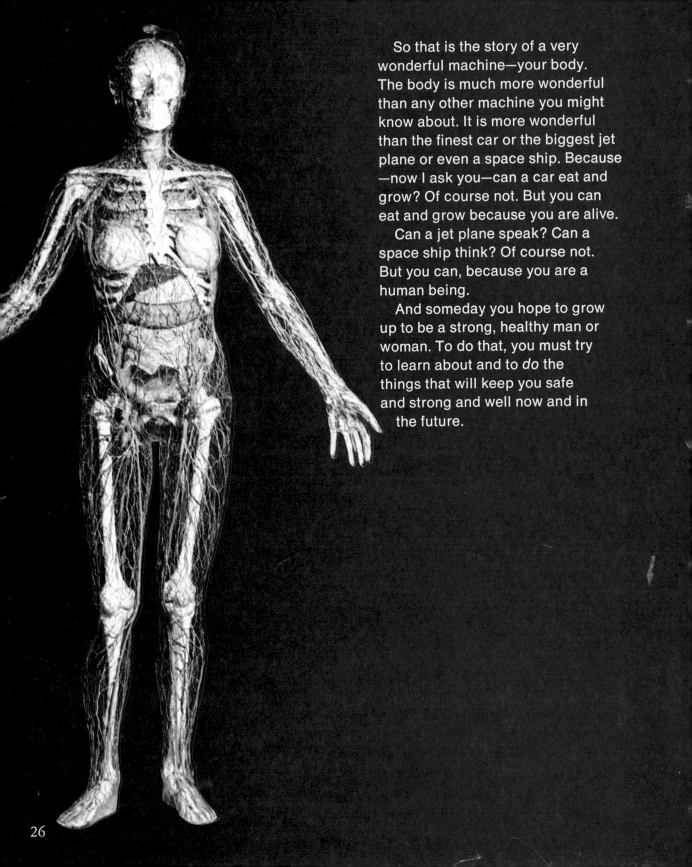

So that is the story of a very wonderful machine—your body. The body is much more wonderful than any other machine you might know about. It is more wonderful than the finest car or the biggest jet plane or even a space ship. Because —now I ask you—can a car eat and grow? Of course not. But you can eat and grow because you are alive.

Can a jet plane speak? Can a space ship think? Of course not. But you can, because you are a human being.

And someday you hope to grow up to be a strong, healthy man or woman. To do that, you must try to learn about and to *do* the things that will keep you safe and strong and well now and in the future.

What Is It?

Now that you have learned about how you look inside, you can check to see how much you remember. Read the riddles below and on page 28 and see if you can answer them.

1. It is the part of you that thinks.
   What is it?

2. They send important messages to your brain, and they give your brain things to think about.
   What are they?

3. Another name for it is your voice box. It helps you talk.
   Its name begins with *l*.
   What is it?

4. When you breathe *in,* air comes into them.
   When you breathe *out,* air goes out of them.
   What are they?

5. It travels to the different parts of your body, and it carries with it food and oxygen the body needs.
   Its name starts with *b*.
   What is it?

6. It works all the time, day and night. It pumps the blood through little tubes to the different parts of your body.
   What is it?

7. It is a large and busy gland. It makes a juice called bile. It stores dissolved sugar from the foods you eat.
   Its name starts with *l*.
   What is it?

8. Some cells inside it help the body use sugar.
   Its name begins with *p*.
   What is it?

9. The food you eat is churned around in this organ.
The food is also mixed with juices as it is churned around.
This organ helps dissolve the food you eat.
What is it?

10. It is a long, narrow tube. If it were stretched out, it would be about 20 feet long.
Digestion is completed in it.
It is the sm__ in__.

11. They stretch out all over your body.
They are fastened to the bones.
They help you move about.
What are they?

12. There are some 200 of them.
They help hold you up.
What are they?

13. They keep the body clean inside.
There are two of them.
They are the k__.

14. It is a small sac.
It stores extra bile.
It is the g__ b__.

15. It mixes with food in your mouth.
It helps dissolve food.
It is s__.

16. It is a waste gas.
When you breathe out, you get rid of it.
It is c__ d__.

What Are Your Questions?

On pages 9 to 26 you learned many things about your body. But no doubt there are still things you want to know. Below are questions some boys and girls your age have asked about the body. Can you answer their questions? Do not write in this book.

1. What are we made of?

2. Why must you get enough sleep?

3. Is there a right way to watch TV?

4. What are tonsils?

5. Why can't you breathe under water?

To see how well you answered the questions, read pages 30 to 39.

Be ready, too, to ask any questions *you* want to have answered about the body or its care.

How might you find answers to your questions?

What Are We Made Of?

You have learned that there are many parts of
you—muscles, fat, nerves, bone, blood, and organs
such as your heart, lungs, stomach, and intestines.

Each part is, in turn, made up of many very tiny
parts. Every tiny part is called a *cell.* These cells are so
very small that you have to use a powerful microscope
to see them. Such a microscope makes the cells look
big enough so that you can see them.

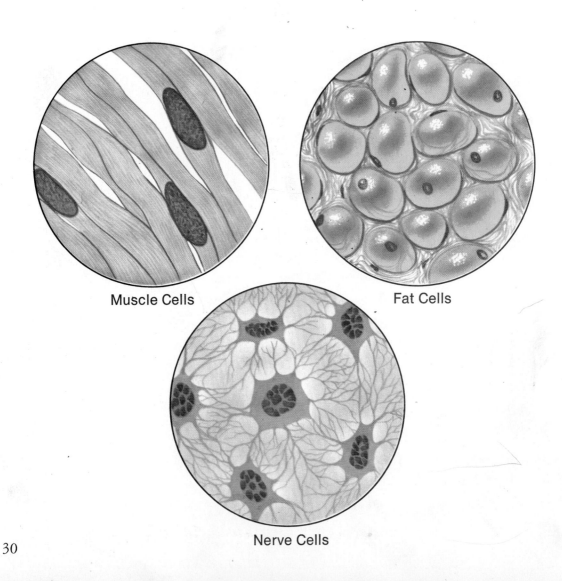

Muscle Cells

Fat Cells

Nerve Cells

When many, many cells of the same kind are grouped together, they make up what is called *tissue*. Many muscle cells make up muscle tissue, many fat cells make up fat tissue, and so on.

If you could look at different kinds of tissue under a powerful microscope, you would see cells like the ones shown here.

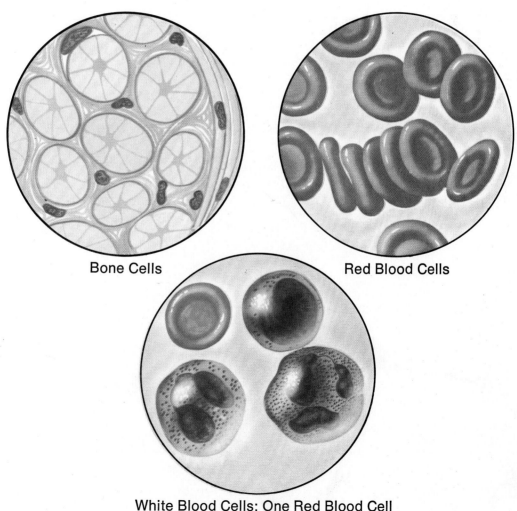

Bone Cells

Red Blood Cells

White Blood Cells; One Red Blood Cell

Did you notice that the fat cells are different from nerve cells, and that muscle cells do not look at all like bone or blood cells? Fat, nerves, muscles, blood, and bone do not look alike, so you would not expect them to be made of the same kinds of cells.

Even though different types of cells do not look alike, they are alike in some important ways. They all have a thin outer cover, or *membrane*.

A Human Cell

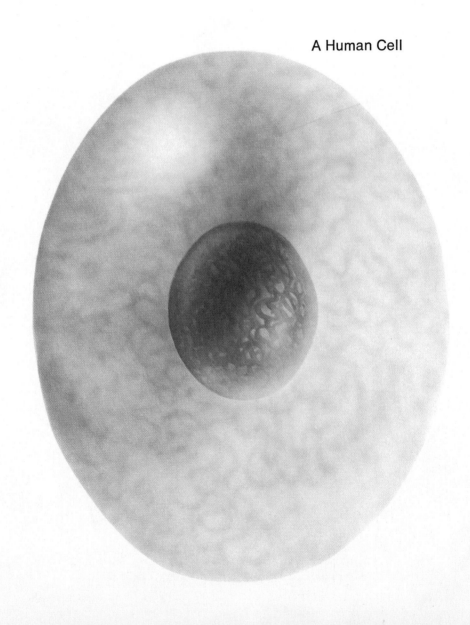

At the center of each cell is a thick part called the *nucleus.* Each cell is made up of a clear, jellylike substance called *protoplasm.*

The cells in your body are alive. They need food and oxygen to keep them living. This food and oxygen is brought to them by the blood that flows round and round through your body.

Most cells can divide and make new cells just like themselves. That is how you grow.

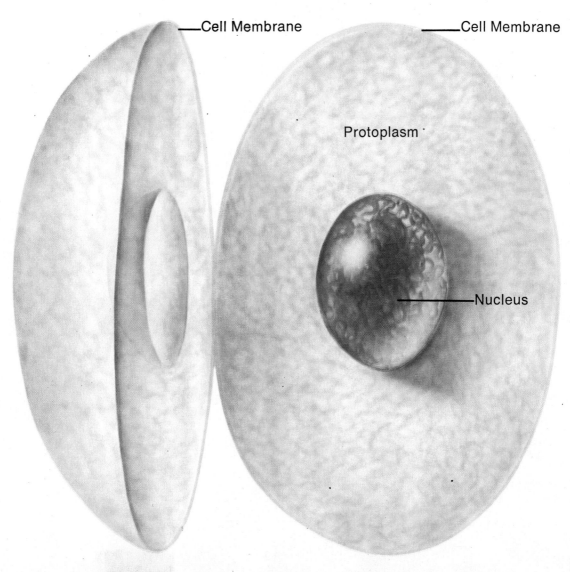

—Cell Membrane

——Cell Membrane

Protoplasm

—Nucleus

Why Must You Get Enough Sleep?

When you are tired and need sleep, your brain may not get the messages from the five main senses as clearly as it should. This may cause you to make many more mistakes than you usually would. You do not think so well when you are very tired as you do when you are rested.

Sometimes when you have not had enough sleep, your muscles are too tired to carry out properly the messages that come to them from your brain. Then accidents may happen.

If you do not get enough sleep, you are also quite likely to feel tired and cross.

Sleep can give you energy for work and play. And it can help keep you strong and healthy. That is why you should try to get the sleep you need. This is about eleven hours each night. Some of you may need more sleep, and others may need a little less.

Is There a Right Way to Watch TV?

It will not tire your eyes to watch television if you practice such good viewing habits as the ones below:

Have a light on in the room when you watch at night; do not look at a bright screen surrounded by darkness.

Sit well back from the TV set—about 8 or 10 feet away.

Look away from the TV screen now and then to rest your eyes.

Look at the TV at eye level, if possible.

Tune in the picture well; a flickering picture can sometimes cause a headache.

Try not to let TV-watching take the place of the outdoor play and exercise you need.

Do not watch the TV set hour after hour just before supper—or for long periods at any time.

Get the sleep you need each night; do not stay up after your bedtime to watch TV.

Keep the noise level down. Watching a program that is tuned in too loud can make you cross or tired or "jittery."

What Are Tonsils?

Tonsils are small organs on each side of the throat at the back of the tongue. They help you by trapping germs, or bacteria, that may enter your body when you breathe. Sometimes they become infected and have to be removed by the doctor.

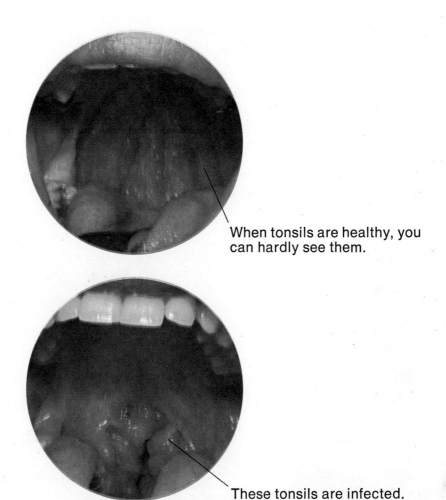

When tonsils are healthy, you can hardly see them.

These tonsils are infected.

Why Can't You Breathe Under Water?

You must have oxygen to stay alive. You get this oxygen from the air you breathe.

There is oxygen in water, too, but your body is not made so that it can separate the oxygen from the water and use it. If you tried to breathe under water, you would find that the lungs could not get the oxygen they need. Then you would drown.

Blue Dots: Carbon Dioxide
Red Dots: Oxygen

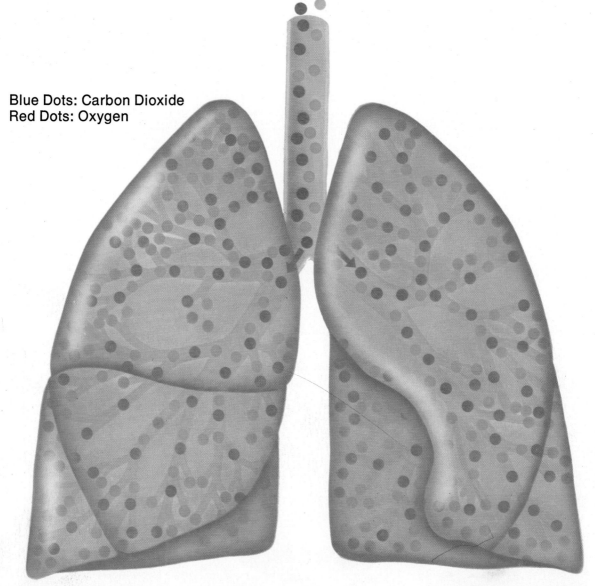

Although *you* cannot breathe under water, a fish
can. A fish can breathe under water because fish and
other sea animals have organs called *gills*. These gills
help sea animals take oxygen from the water. But
if the sea animals are taken out of the water, their
gills dry out. They cannot take oxygen from the
air and they soon die.

If you could look inside a fish gill,
you would find that it looks like this.

Things to Do

1. You might sketch a rough outline of the body and put in some of the important organs, such as the brain, liver, heart, lungs, and stomach. A class committee might choose some of the drawings to put on the bulletin board.

2. Some of you may want to try putting together a homemade stethoscope. Use two narrow rubber tubes—each one about two feet long. Put one end of each rubber tube into a small funnel and the free ends of the rubber tubes into your ears. Then you can use the stethoscope to hear your own heartbeat.

3. Breathe *out* all the air you can, and then have someone use a tape measure to check the size of your chest.

   Next breathe *in* as much air as you can, and have the size of your chest measured again.

   What happens to the size of your chest during breathing?

4. Tell why your body is often called a wonderful machine.

5. An interesting book about how people like you may someday live and work under the sea is *You Will Live Under the Sea* by F. and M. Phleger. Look for this book at the library.

6. Tell how the brain gets things to think about.

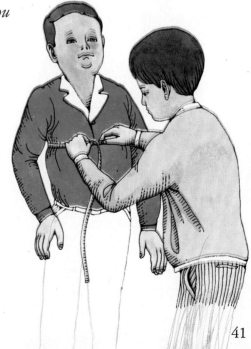

Checking Up

What Is It?

On a piece of paper write the numbers from 1 to 10. Beside each number write the name for each of these parts:

1. Part of the body that pumps blood through blood vessels.
2. The voice box.
3. Juice in the mouth that starts to digest food.
4. Parts of the body that are fastened to bones and that help you move.
5. Part of the body that thinks.
6. Parts of the body that always have air in them.
7. Part of the body that churns and mixes food and helps dissolve the food.
8. The tiny parts your body is made of —so tiny they can only be seen with a powerful microscope.
9. A large, busy gland that makes bile.
10. Nerves that carry messages to the brain from the sense organs.

Yes or No?

Now write the numbers from 11 to 18 on your paper. Beside each number write the answer to each question, *yes* or *no.*

11. Do all the cells in your body look alike?
12. Do you have muscles in your legs?
13. Are tonsils found in your toes?
14. Can sleep give you energy for work and play?
15. Should you sit 8 to 10 feet back from your TV set?
16. Can your lungs take oxygen from water?
17. Does your brain have bone around it to help keep it safe?
18. Can you see a human cell without using a microscope?

Number of Answers   18
Number Right

2 How Can You Prevent Accidents?

Learning How to Prevent Accidents

Most accidents can be prevented. But to prevent accidents, you must first know about safe things to do. Then you must be able to *use* what you know at the right time.

This unit will help you check your safety knowledge. But YOU are the one to make sure you put your knowledge to use.

When you put your safety knowledge to use, you can often avoid doing unsafe things—things that can hurt you or others. As you know, being thoughtful of others includes thinking about *their* safety, too.

As you study this unit, see if you can think of times when you have put your safety knowledge to use.

What Do You Check on a Bicycle?

Do you know how to make a bicycle-safety check?

What things do you think the boys in the picture at the right should check on the bicycle?

Now turn the page. There you will see a poem that gives clues about what should be looked for when a bicycle-safety check is made.

The answer:

In the poem below you can find answers to the question on page 44 about a bicycle-safety check.

Be ready to tell the main "check points" on a bicycle.

Boy with a Bike

Brakes?
    Just right, for every use.
Chain?
    Not tight, yet not too loose.
Tires?
    O.K. Correct for air.
Pedal treads?
    In good repair.
Handlebars?
    They're straight and tight.
Grips on handlebars?
    Quite right.
Light? Reflector?
    Working fine.
Saddle?
    Firm and right in line.
Pump? And tools?
    All there. Heigh-ho!
    Everything is set . . .
    LET'S GO.

Reprinted from *Health and Safety Plays and Programs*, by Aileen Fisher. Plays, Inc., Publishers, Boston, Mass. 02116. Copyright © 1953 by Aileen Fisher.

What Will You Check?

If you were coming out of your driveway on your way to school one morning, like the girl at the right, would you know how to ride safely? Check yourself to see.

On which side of the road would you ride?

How would you carry books or packages?

Now look on page 48 to check your answers.

The answer:

Check both ways for traffic before coming out into the street. Always ride at the right-hand edge of the road. A good driver rides *with* traffic. If rules in your community say you should ride on the sidewalk, you must do so. If you ride on the sidewalk, you still should keep to the right.

When you cross at a corner, always get off your bike and walk it across. If there are crosswalks, be sure to use them.

Carry your books or packages in a basket or carrier. You need both hands to keep your balance. If you do not have a basket or carrier, tie your books or packages to the frame of your bicycle.

What Signals Are Used?

Look at the girl on the bike at the right.

What signal should she give if she wants to STOP?

What signal should she give if she wants to make a left turn?

What signal should she give if she wants to make a right turn?

Suppose that you and your friend both have bikes and you are riding together. How would you ride?

What would you do if you *had* to be out on your bicycle at dusk some night?

Now check your answers with the ideas given on page 50.

The answer:

Be sure to give correct signals—and in plenty of time—when you turn or stop. The pictures below show the correct signals for a stop, a left turn, and a right turn.

Ride single file. If your friend has a bike and you ride together, one should ride in front of the other. Always keep a distance of at least a bicycle-length between you. Be sure to ride in a straight line. Never zigzag. And never hitch a ride on a car or truck.

Do all your riding in the daytime if you can. But if you *must* be out at dusk or at night, be sure you have a white light in front and a red reflector, tail light, or reflector tapes at the rear. And at night you should wear something white or light-colored—or something that shines in the dark—so that you can be seen easily.

Remember, too, traffic lights and signs are for bike drivers as well as car drivers. You must watch for the traffic lights and signs and obey them!

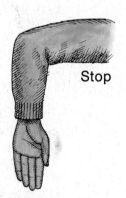 

Stop   Left Turn   Right Turn

What Should You Do?

Suppose it is a rainy day and you decide you and your friend might as well play a game indoors.

High on a shelf in your closet is a game you want. What should you do to reach the game?

Use the picture at the right to help you discuss this question. Then check your answer with page 52.

The answer:

When you want to reach something in a high place, the best thing to do is to use a stepladder or a stepstool. Or you might stand on a very sturdy chair. Many falls occur when people stand on rickety chairs, rocking chairs, or stools that tip over easily. Another thing you might do is ask a tall member of your family to reach the object for you.

There are other ways to avoid falls, too. Some guides are given below. See if you can think of some good reasons for each safety guide.

Keep toys and books off stairs.

Walk, don't run, in the house or in school halls.

Use the handrail, if possible, when going up and down stairs.

Wipe up at once any liquids that are spilled.

Put ashes or sand on slippery walks or steps.

Tie your shoelaces if they become untied.

What Do You Do in a Fire Drill?

Suppose you are at work in your classroom when the fire signal sounds. What would you do to get out of the classroom and the school building safely?

Use the picture at the right to help you discuss this question. Then compare your ideas with the ones on page 54.

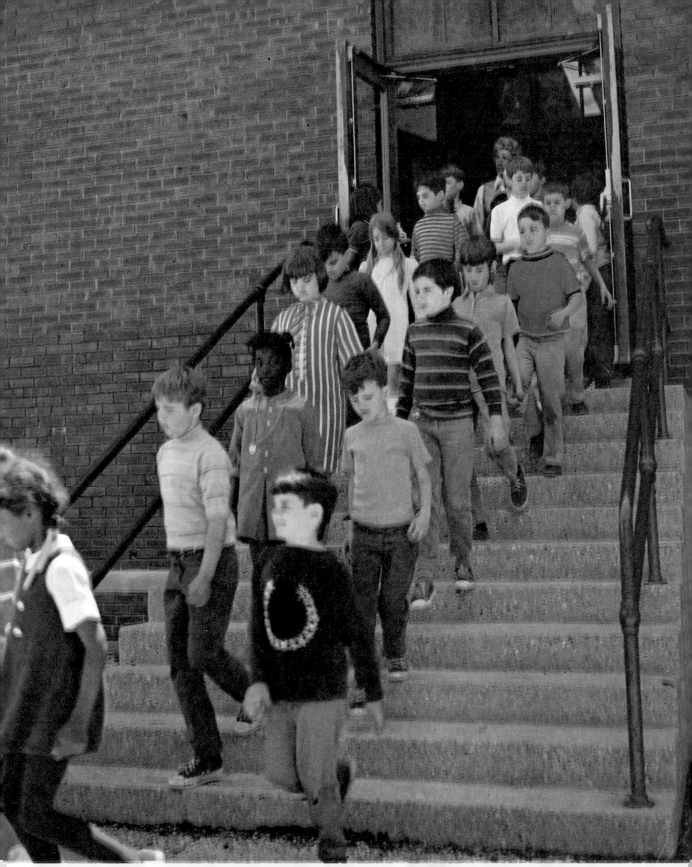

The answer:

The best thing to do in a fire drill is to get out of the building quickly. When the fire signal sounds, line up with your class and walk out quickly and quietly, as you have been taught to do.

Keeping quiet during a fire drill is important so that you can hear any directions that may be given.

If you are in the washroom when the fire signal sounds, walk out with the first class you see. When you have reached a safe area, ask the teacher of that class if you can go find your own class.

If you and the others in your class are on the playground when the fire signal sounds, get into line quickly. Then walk quickly away from the school as you always do in fire drills.

How Do You Keep Safe Around Water?

Suppose you have gone to the beach for a swim, like the boys in the picture at the right.

What are some safe things you must think about when you go swimming?

Turn to page 56 and check your answers with the ones given there.

The answer:

Did you think about any of these things when you were deciding about keeping safe around water?

Swim only where there is a lifeguard.

Never swim alone; have a friend or "buddy" with you.

If you cannot swim, stay out of deep water.

Swim only when you are feeling well—not when you are tired, chilled, overheated, or are just recovering from an illness.

Never jokingly call for help in the water.

What reasons can you think of for each of the guides given above?

How Can Signs Help Keep You Safe?

Suppose you are walking to the store one day and on the way you see a sign like the one shown in the picture at the right.

How could such a sign help keep you safe?

Where might you see signs like this one?

Now turn to page 58 to find out more about signs that you should be sure to read and obey.

The answer:

The safety signs you see about you every day can help you by warning you of possible danger. The construction sign on page 57, for example, is the kind used near a building or something that is being built but is not yet finished. There may be holes or loose boards in a floor or nails sticking up somewhere. Or there may be heavy machinery at work. You can guess, can't you, how these things might be dangerous?

Other warning signs you may sometimes see are NO TRESPASSING and BEWARE OF DOG signs. These signs mean *stay away* or *do not come in here.*

The RAILROAD CROSSING sign is another safety sign. It warns you to look out for trains and to wait until they have passed before you cross the tracks.

Try to remember to watch for such signs, to read them, and to obey them.

How Do You Use a Toaster Safely?

Suppose you are going to help your mother get breakfast in the morning, as the girl is doing at the right. Your mother asks you to make the toast.

What are some things you should remember to do when you plug in, or unplug, the toaster?

How will you remove toast from the toaster?

Check your answers with those on page 60.

The answer:

When you are plugging in a toaster or other piece of electric equipment, remember that its electric cord has a handle on it. Use this handle when you plug a cord into an outlet or when you unplug it. In this way you will avoid any chance of an electric shock.

If a piece of toast should get stuck in the toaster, *unplug* the toaster before you attempt to dig out the toast with something metal like a fork. Electricity travels through metal and you could get a bad electric shock.

Keep in mind, too, that when your hands are wet, it is easy for an electric current to come into your body through your skin. So be sure your hands are dry when you are using electric equipment in the kitchen or in any other room of the house.

How Do You Keep Safe on the Playground?

Suppose your class goes out to the playground. Some of your friends want to play on the overhead ladders. What are some things to remember about playing on overhead ladders or other playground equipment?

Use the picture at the right to discuss the question. Then check your ideas with those on page 62.

The answer:

There are guides you can use to keep safe on playground equipment. For example, when climbing on or off equipment, check to be sure that no one is behind you so you will not kick him or her. Also avoid playing near the area where the swings are.

If there are rings for stretching and for pulling yourself up, you can be careful to use only your hands in them. Do not hang by your knees. Why?

Another way to avoid accidents on playground equipment is to stay off it when it is wet. When wet, the equipment is slippery; then falls are more likely to occur. Warn your friends about this also.

You may be able to think of still other safety guides for using playground equipment. What are some of *your* safety guides?

How Can You Be Safe in Running Games?

Suppose you and some friends are playing a tag game in which you have to run, like the boys and girls in the picture at the right. Can you think of some things you can do to help avoid accidents during the game?

Now compare your ideas with those on page 64.

The answer:

One of the first things to remember when several players are running in a game is to try to spread out. In this way runners do not bump into one another or trip each other. Often accidents occur when the players "bunch up" and do not remember to keep enough space between themselves and others.

Something else to remember is this: If your shoelace should come untied, you should immediately drop out of the game to tie it.

It also helps in running games if you have on tennis shoes or rubber-soled shoes that will help keep you from slipping and falling.

On Which Side of the Car Do You Get Out?

Suppose you and your family have just driven up to the grocery store. Your father stops the car and asks you to go into the store to get a loaf of bread. You are sitting in the back seat just behind your father who is driving, like the boy shown in the picture at the right.

On which side of the car would you get out?

Now compare your answer with that on page 66.

The answer:

To avoid being hit by a car in the street, always
get out of your car on the *curb side*. You may have to
crawl over another passenger in the car to do it.
Or you may have to slide across the seat. But getting
out on the curb side is the only safe way to leave a
car if it is parked on a street.

There are other safe things for car riders to do.
Some of these things are shown below. See if you can
explain why each one is a safe thing to do.

Lock the car doors.

Fasten your safety belts.

Keep your head, hands, and arms inside the car.

Avoid doing anything that might disturb the
driver of the car.

Do You Have to Take a Dare?

Suppose there is an old, empty house near
where you live, such as the one shown at the
right. A friend dares you to go into it.

Would you take the dare? Why or why not?

Do you always have to take a dare? Are there
some dares that are safe to take?

Turn to page 68 to find out.

The answer:

Did you decide that there are two kinds of dares—some you can take and some you cannot?

One kind of dare you should not take is one that is *unsafe* and that might cause someone to get hurt. For example, in an old, abandoned house you might get cut on glass from a broken window. Or you might fall through a rotted floor or step on some old nails. What is more, it is not only unsafe to play in abandoned houses, it is against the law.

Some other places that are unsafe for children to play in or near, and that should always be avoided, are city dumps, railroad yards, quarries, caves, and gravel pits.

Only foolish people feel that they have to take unsafe dares. They might take the dare because they don't want to seem afraid. But a boy or girl may be a lot braver to *refuse* an unsafe dare than to take it. Only foolish people *make* unsafe dares!

You are growing up now and are able to tell when a dare is unsafe. Watch out for dares about taking strange pills or trying another person's medicine or sniffing deeply such things as glue. These are unsafe dares that could be dangerous to your health.

There is another kind of dare that is harmless and that is made just for fun. You can take this kind of dare.

Can you think of a safe dare? What is it?

Can you think of an unsafe dare? Why is it unsafe?

Do You Remember?

For several years you have been learning about safe things to do. Check yourself to see how many of these important things you remember.

1. How can you make sure it is safe for you to get into a bathtub or shower?
2. What are the only safe places for crossing streets?
3. What should you do if a stranger asks you to go for a ride in a car?
4. Suppose you meet a strange dog on the sidewalk and the dog growls at you. What should you do?
5. Suppose you are going on a class trip in the school bus. What safety ideas will you keep in mind on the trip?
6. Pretend you are a policeman. Be ready to give the policeman's STOP signal and the GO AHEAD signal.
7. Be ready to show how to give these signals if you are riding a bicycle: STOP, LEFT TURN, RIGHT TURN.
8. What are some safe ways to play with a rope?
9. What should you do if your clothes catch fire?

Things to Do

1. Look at the poster at the right. Be ready to tell what it means when you are walking or riding on roads.

2. Now you make a safety poster. You might make it about fire safety, safety when swimming, or safety on the playground.

3. See if you can fill in the missing words:
   When you sit in the car, look
   for the ____ ____, and be
   sure to fasten them!

4. Make up a second rhyming line here:
   If you ride a bike at night,

   _____.

5. Read the facts below and then think of a safety message for the sign in the picture at the right:

   Men are working behind this fence.
   There are trucks and big machines.
   There is a deep ditch.
   Children should stay away from here.

   What message might be put on the sign?

More Things to Do

1. Be ready to tell or write about a safe thing you have done today—or about a safe thing you have seen someone else do.
2. Talk to your mother about some of the things she does at home to help keep the family safe.
3. Talk to your father—and your mother, too, if she also has a job away from home—about the ways people are kept safe where they work.
4. Tell or write about an accident that has happened lately to you or to someone you know. Explain how you think the accident might have been avoided.
5. Be ready to act out something safe to do when you are riding a bicycle. See if the others can guess what you are doing.
6. Make a list of things to remember during a fire drill. Post the list in your classroom.
7. Unscramble these safety messages:

   TSOP

   REGDAN

   EEPK OT IGHRT

   ITXE

Checking Up

Fill In the Missing Words

Copy each sentence on your paper and fill in the missing word or words. Do not write in this book.

1. If you and a friend are on bikes and riding together, be sure to ride s__ f__.

2. If you are riding a bike on a street or road, keep to the r__.

3. Be sure to use both h__ to steer your bicycle.

4. Swim only in places that are protected by a l__g__rd.

5. NO TRESPASSING means st__ aw__ or k__ o__.

6. Never go swimming all by y__.

7. In a fire drill, walk out q__ly and q__ly.

8. When you are in the water, you should never jokingly call for h__.

9. If you are on a bike, you should *never* h__ a ride on a c__ or a tr__.

10. If you cannot swim, stay out of d__ w__.

11. To reach something on a high shelf, use a stepl__ or a steps__.

12. When you plug an electric cord into an outlet, always use the h__.

Number of Answers   12

Number Right   _____

3 How Much Do You Know About Your Teeth and Their Care?

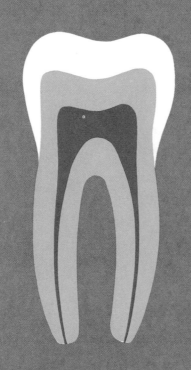

What Are Primary Teeth?

In the past few years you have learned something about your primary teeth.

You may have learned that you had all your primary teeth by the time you were two or three years old. Of course, children differ a lot in the age at which these teeth come through the jaw.

You can learn more about your primary teeth by looking at the picture on page 75.

How many teeth are in the primary set?

How many primary molars are there?

Children differ, too, in the ages at which they lose, or *shed,* the primary teeth. But there are timetables that tell when these teeth usually come out. Look at the timetable shown on page 75.

Which are the first of the primary teeth to be shed?

Which primary teeth are shed around the ages of seven and eight?

Which are the last primary teeth to be shed? At what ages are they shed?

Some boys and girls your age think the primary teeth are not very important. These children think, "I'm going to lose all my primary teeth and get my permanent teeth some day. So it doesn't really matter if I don't take care of my primary teeth. And it doesn't matter if my primary teeth get cavities in them and have to be pulled before they come out naturally." What do *you* think about the primary teeth and the need to take care of them?

About when primary teeth are shed:

Central Incisor	7½ Years
Lateral Incisor	8 Years
Cuspid	11½ Years
First Molar	10½ Years
Second Molar	10½ Years

Second Molar	11 Years
First Molar	10 Years
Cuspid	9½ Years
Lateral Incisor	7 Years
Central Incisor	6 Years

Why Do You Need Your Primary Teeth?

Do you think it is important to take good care of your primary teeth and to try to keep them until it is time for them to come out? If so, you are right.

Your primary teeth have important jobs to do, and they should be kept in your mouth until they are lost naturally.

For one thing, your primary teeth are needed for chewing. As you have learned, food begins to be digested in the mouth when it is chewed and mixed with saliva. If primary teeth come out before they are ready to be replaced by permanent teeth, the food cannot be chewed well.

You need your primary teeth to help you talk, too—just as you will later need your permanent teeth. If you lose too many of your teeth before you should, it will be hard for you to say clearly words with the sounds of such letters as *f, g, j,* and *s* in them.

Your primary teeth are also needed to be guides for the permanent teeth that are forming under them. If primary teeth are missing, they cannot guide the permanent teeth into their right places. Notice in the picture chart below how the primary teeth are guides for the permanent teeth forming under them.

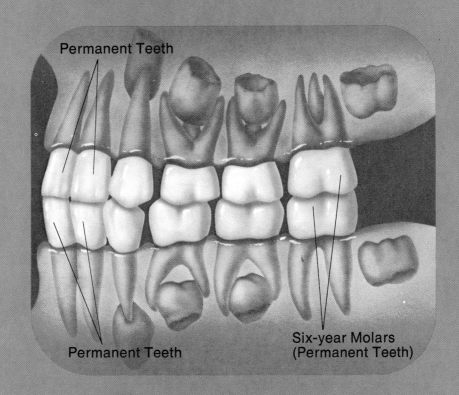

Permanent Teeth

Permanent Teeth

Six-year Molars
(Permanent Teeth)

What If a Primary Tooth Is Lost Too Soon?

There is still another reason why primary teeth should be given good care and kept in your mouth until it is time for them to be shed. When a primary tooth comes out too soon, the teeth at each side of it may move over and fill part of the space that is left. Then there will not be enough room for the permanent tooth. It cannot grow in its proper place if there is not enough space for it. That is what you see happening in the picture below.

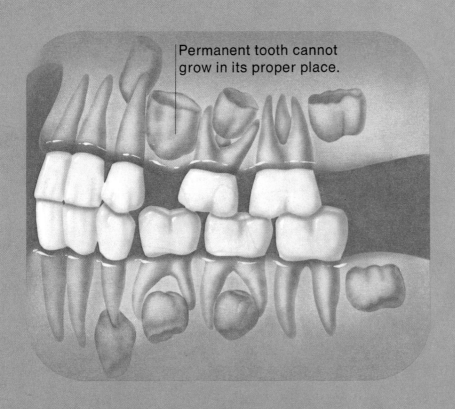

Permanent tooth cannot grow in its proper place.

What Are Space Maintainers?

To keep primary teeth from moving into the space where a permanent tooth will come through, the dentist may use a wire *space maintainer*. You can see a space maintainer in the picture below. When the permanent tooth starts to come through, the dentist takes off the space maintainer.

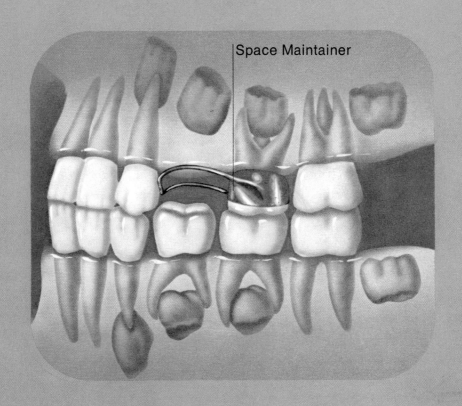

Space Maintainer

What Are the Parts of a Tooth?

When you look at a tooth in your mouth, you see only part of the tooth. You see only the *crown.* The crown is the part above the *gum,* or the fleshy tissue around the teeth.

But you cannot see the *roots* of your teeth. The roots are below the gums. An *incisor* and a *cuspid*—which cut and tear food—have just one root each. But a *molar*—which grinds food—has two or three roots. Roots fasten teeth to the jawbone. Before a primary tooth gets loose, its roots *dissolve.* Then a primary tooth sheds easily.

Incisor   Cuspid   Molar

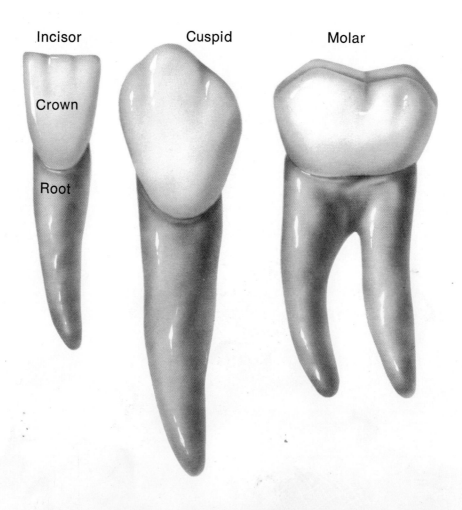

Crown

Root

What Are Your Questions About Teeth?

So far you have learned some interesting things about your teeth. What have you learned that you did not know before?

There may be other things you would like to know about the teeth, too.

Below you can see questions that some boys and girls your age have asked about the teeth. How would you answer these questions?

Check your answers with the ones given on pages 82 to 87.

1. How can we keep from getting cavities?

2. How does the dentist fill a cavity?

3. Can a knocked-out tooth be replaced?

4. How should you brush your teeth?

5. How many permanent teeth are there?

What are some questions that you have about the teeth? How might you find answers to your questions?

Did you think of talking to the school nurse? Did you think about using books in the library? What other ways did you think of for finding answers?

How Can We Keep from Getting Cavities?

No one thing will prevent cavities—or *dental caries* as they are called—in the teeth. But there are some things that can help.

Children who drink water containing a very small amount of a *chemical* called *fluoride* get fewer cavities than do other children. In some communities this fluoride is present naturally in the drinking water. Other communities add fluoride to the drinking water. Does your community do this?

You can help prevent dental caries by brushing your teeth after meals and after eating sweets.

82

Regular visits to the dentist help, too. The dentist has special tools for cleaning your teeth well. In the picture at the left below you can see some scalers, for cleaning tartar off the teeth; a hand mirror; part of a jet spray; and a dentist's mixing bowl. If you can, you should visit the dentist two times a year, or as often as he advises it.

You can also help by choosing snacks like the ones at the right below and by cutting down on the sweet snacks you eat. Sweet, sticky foods, like candy and cake, help cause cavities.

How Does the Dentist Fill a Cavity?

When the dentist finds a cavity in a tooth, he uses a special tool to clean out the decayed part of the tooth. This is to make the cavity ready for filling.

If the cavity is deep, the dentist may inject a medicine to keep you from feeling uncomfortable.

When the cavity is ready to be filled, the dentist puts in a filling of plastic or silver or some other material.

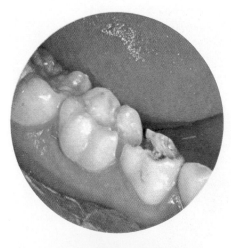

Cavities in two teeth next to each other have been cleaned out by the dentist.

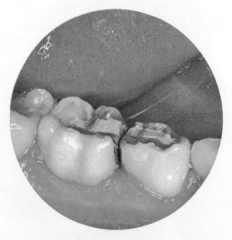

The dentist has taken care of the cavities in the two teeth by filling them.

Can a Knocked-out Tooth Be Replaced?

If a tooth is knocked out of your jaw, you can sometimes have it replaced. This is what you should do. Put the knocked-out tooth in a wet cloth or paper handkerchief and hurry home with it. See if your mother or father can take you and the tooth to a dentist right away. The dentist knows how to put the tooth back so that it is likely to stay in place.

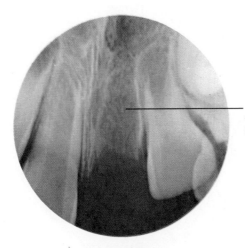

A front tooth was lost in an accident.

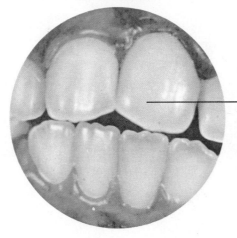

The dentist put the tooth back in place. He fastened the tooth to the ones next to it, so the replaced tooth could grow into the jawbone again.

How Should You Brush Your Teeth?

When you brush your teeth, you want to be sure to brush away the bits of food that cling to them.

A good way to brush your teeth is shown below. Remember to hold the toothbrush alongside the teeth. Tip the brush against the gum line. Brush back and forth, back and forth.

When you brush your teeth well, you help remove bits of food and *plaque*. Plaque is a sticky, colorless film of harmful germs which is always forming on the teeth. If you remove the plaque, you can help keep cavities from forming.

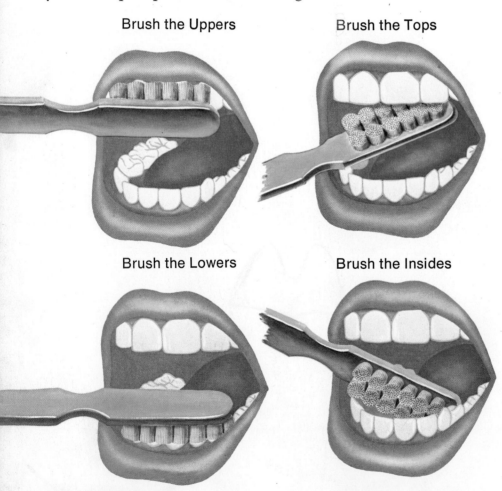

Brush the Uppers   Brush the Tops

Brush the Lowers   Brush the Insides

How Many Permanent Teeth Are There?

The picture below shows the teeth that make up your second, or permanent, set of teeth. How many permanent teeth are there in all?

Your permanent teeth are supposed to last a lifetime. You can help keep them by taking care of them.

Be sure to brush them *well* at least once a day. If you can, use dental floss to remove plaque and bits of food from between the teeth. Avoid eating sweet, sticky foods between meals. See your dentist for regular checkups.

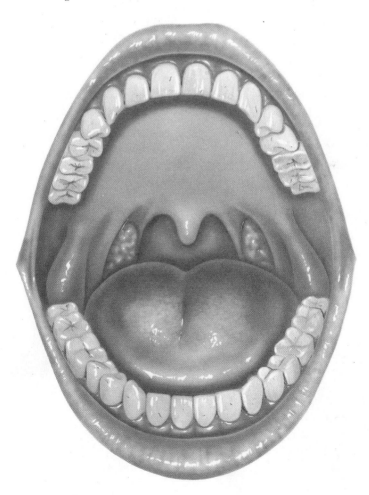

Do You Remember?

From this book and from other books you have studied in the last few years you have learned many things about your teeth and their care. The questions below will help you see how much you remember. Answer each question as best you can.

1. Why should you brush your teeth?
2. When should you brush your teeth?
3. What is a good thing to do to remove plaque and bits of food from between the teeth?
4. How many primary teeth do you have?
5. What are some tools a dentist uses?
6. What is another name for the second teeth?
7. What are the first teeth of your second set?
8. What are the parts of the teeth?
9. How many permanent teeth are there in all?

Things to Do

1. See if you can answer this question: If a primary tooth comes out naturally, why can't you see its root?

2. The girl you see in the picture on this page is in the dentist's office. Tell what you know about the different things you see in the picture.

3. Tell about some ways in which permanent teeth are different from primary teeth.

4. Make a poster that tells one good way to help take care of your teeth.

5. Use a hand mirror to look at your teeth. Try to find a six-year molar. Look for the sixth tooth back from the front center. Tell what you know about six-year molars.

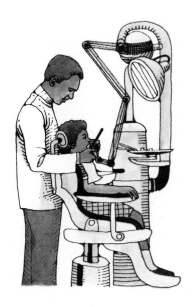

Checking Up

Fill In the Missing Word

Copy sentences 1 to 7 on your paper and fill in the word or words or number that is missing.

1. Two main parts of a tooth are the __ and the __.
2. There are __ teeth in the primary set.
3. There are __ teeth in the permanent set.
4. You can help prevent cavities by cutting down on the __, __ foods you eat.
5. You need your teeth to __ your food.
6. Your first permanent teeth are the six-year __.
7. Use dental __ to remove plaque.

Yes or No?

Copy the numbers from 8 to 12 on your paper. After each number write the correct answer, *yes* or *no.*

8. Are the six-year-molars at the front of the mouth?
9. Do permanent teeth form in the jaw under the primary teeth?
10. Can a knocked-out tooth sometimes be replaced?
11. Do you have all of your permanent teeth by age eight?
12. Is it important to try to keep the primary teeth until they are ready to come out naturally?

Number of Answers   12
Number Right   ____

4 How Can You Move About?

A Poem About Dancing

A hop, a skip, and off you go!
Happy heart and merry toe.

Up-and-down and in-and-out,
This way, that way, round about!

Bend like grasses in the breeze,
Wave your arms like wind-blown trees!

Dart like swallows, glide like fish,
Dance like anything you wish.

Soundless as the snowflakes white,
Swift as shooting-stars at night.

Nimble as a goblin-elf,
Dance, dance, and be yourself.

Stately, sprightly, so and so
 Quick and slow,
 To and fro.

Kicking high and jumping low,
A skip, a hop, and off you go!

"Dancing" from *Poems for Children* by Eleanor Farjeon. Copyright 1938 by Eleanor Farjeon; Copyright renewed 1966 by Gervase Farjeon. Published by J. B. Lippincott Company. Reprinted by permission of the publisher and David Higham Associates, Ltd.

How Would You Move?

In the poem at the left you read of many ways to move about. What are some of these ways?

Which of these movements can you use to move your whole body from one place to another?

Which of these movements can you do while you stay in place?

Can you show how you would "dart" like a swallow?

Can you show how you would "glide" like a fish?

How would you move about in a "stately" way? In a "sprightly" way? (If you do not know the meaning of each word, look it up in the Glossary.)

Be ready to show how you would *kick high* and *jump low*. Also show how you would *skip* or *hop* fast, then slow, then fast again.

What Helps You Move About?

Do you know why you can skip and hop and bend and twist as you move about? You can do these and many other movements because of the way your body is made.

Your skeleton has bending places, or joints, in it. Joints are places where one bone ends and another bone begins.

The muscles that are fastened to your bones also help you move about. The pictures show the wall of muscles in your *trunk*. Your trunk is the part of your body from your shoulders to the top of your legs.

...muscles of the trunk bend easily and they help ...nd forward and backward and sideways.

...e the large, strong muscles in the back of the ...hese muscles hold your backbone straight, ...y help you make powerful movements like ...u use in batting a ball.

...are strong muscles in your neck as well. ...rong neck muscles help you twist and turn ...d.

95

Do you know why you can bend your arms and then straighten them? It is because you have long, strong muscles in your arms.

To make a bone move, muscles usually work in pairs. One muscle *contracts,* or becomes shorter and thicker, while the other *relaxes,* or stretches out. This pulls one bone toward another.

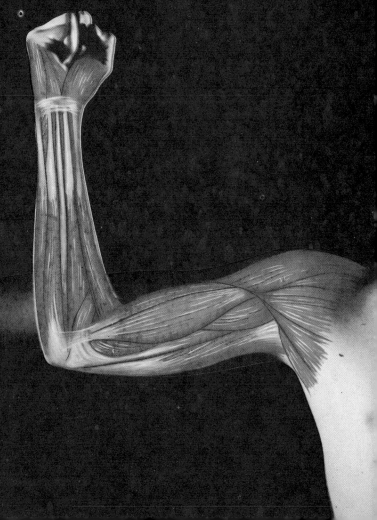

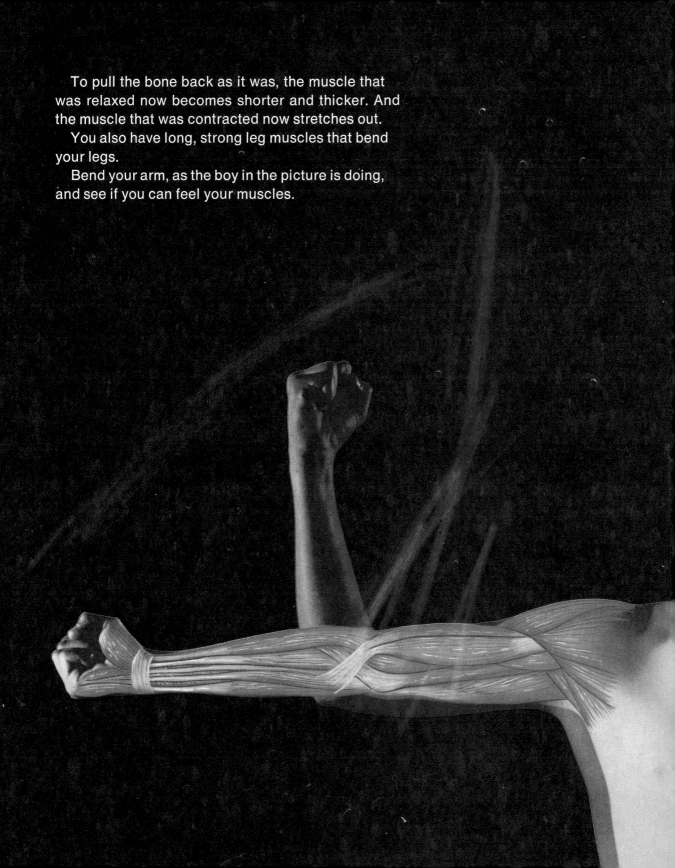

To pull the bone back as it was, the muscle that was relaxed now becomes shorter and thicker. And the muscle that was contracted now stretches out.

You also have long, strong leg muscles that bend your legs.

Bend your arm, as the boy in the picture is doing, and see if you can feel your muscles.

What Are Locomotor Movements?

Suppose you are asked to move from one side of the playground to the other. How would *you* move?

These movements that take you from one place to another are called *locomotor movements*.

How many *different* ways can you think of to move from one place to another?

Leap   Hop   Skip

Did you think of ways of moving that are shown on these two pages?

Have you ever used any of these movements to play a game?

On the next two pages, you can read about a game that uses some of these locomotor movements.

Slide   Jump   Gallop

A Relay Race: Locomotor Movements

Two or more teams can play this relay race.

Players on each team line up behind the starting line.

At the signal *"Go,"* the first one in each line *runs* to the jumping rope. He picks up the rope. He *jumps* the rope two times; then he drops the rope to the ground.

He *hops* on to touch a line drawn about five feet beyond the rope.

Next he *skips* back to his team.

The first one back wins a point for his team.

The game goes on until each player has a chance to be in the Run-Jump-Hop-Skip Relay. The team with the most points wins.

What Are Nonlocomotor Movements?

Suppose you are asked to see how many ways you can move while a part of your body—such as one leg —stays in one place. What are some things you would do?

Movements you can make while a part of you stays in one place are called *nonlocomotor movements.*

Be ready to show as many ways as you can of moving while part of you stays in place.

Can you think of times when you have used some nonlocomotor movements?

Look at the next two pages to see some nonlocomotor activities.

Can You Do These Things?

Bend down and try to touch your toes with your fingertips. Keep your legs slightly bent at the knees.

Then straighten up.

Do this three or four times.

Keep feet together and lift your arms. Count as you circle your arms *forward* first in small circles; then gradually make larger circles until you reach the count of ten. Relax. Now circle your arms *backward*.

Keep feet apart and clasp hands
behind head.
  Twist left, twist right.
Left, right. Left, right.
Count to ten.

Kick high in place with one foot.
Do it ten times.
  Now do the same thing with the
other foot.

What Can You Do to Have Good Posture?

When people talk about posture, they are talking about the way a person sits and stands and walks.

You look better when you have good posture.

Also when you have good posture, you can work and play without getting tired too soon.

Which picture below shows good sitting posture?
Where should the boy's back be?

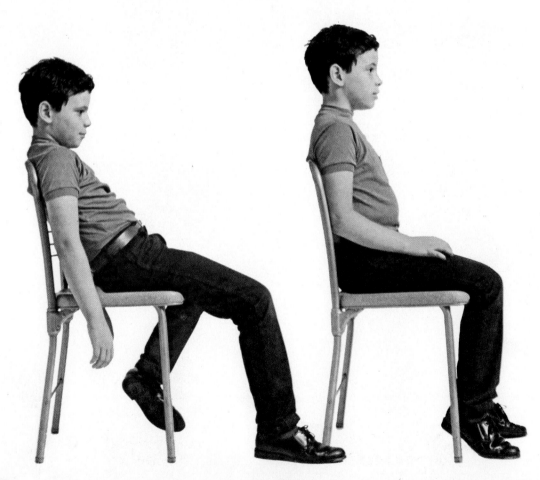

106

Which picture below shows good standing posture?
What makes you think so?

Are You a Good Sport?

Do you know what it means to be a "good sport"?
How would you explain it?

Now see what is happening in the picture below.
Do you see anyone here who needs to know more
about being a good sport? Who is it?

Plan to act out what could happen because this
boy is being a bad sport. Then act out what would
happen if this boy were a better sport.

"This ball is *mine,* and
if you want to play with it,
you'll have to let me bat
right now! Come on, give
me the bat!"

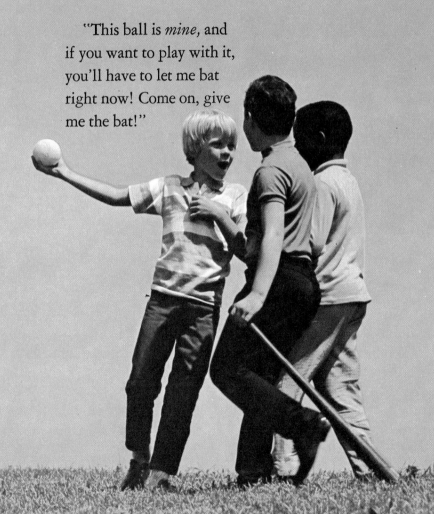

Now look at the picture at the bottom of this page. Sally and her friends are playing jump rope.

Jumping rope is hard for Sally, and she often trips on the rope.

Are her friends good sports about it? What makes you think so?

"Come on, Sally. We'll help you. Run in when the rope is up, and be ready to jump when it comes down."

Things to Do

1. Read the poem on page 111.
   See if you can make an X with your body.
   Now try making the letter Y.
   Try to make yourself into the letter Z, too.
2. Can you make the letter C with your body?
   Try it.
3. Can you use some parts of your body to make
   the letter O? Try it.
4. What do you see here?
   Can you walk in a circle?
   Can you run in a circle?
   Can you move backward in a circle?
   Show how you would do these things.
5. What do you see here?
   Can you hop in this shape?
   Can you skip in this shape?
   Show how you would do these things.
6. Can you spell your first name while hopping
   on the floor? While walking? While sliding?
   Can you take up lots of space while you spell it?
   Can you take up only a little space?

Activities on this page adapted by permission of the publisher from *A Guide to Movement Exploration* by Layne C. Hackett and Robert G. Jenson. Copyright © 1967 by Peek Publications.

I'm very fond of X,
He's such a little mark.
He crosses in the middle
Like a pathway in the park.

Y holds his hands above his head,
And never lets them drop,
I know when I have come to Y,
It's almost time to stop.

Poor zigzag Z's the very last,
He's awfully far away,
I really should be nice to him
And put him up with A.

From "Fun from A to Z" by Frances S. Copley
from *Child Life*, Copyright © 1961. Reprinted by
permission of Child Life.

More Things to Do

1. What is the first letter of your first name? Can you walk that letter pattern?

2. Can you hop in the pattern of the word "hop"? Show how you would do it.

3. Can you skip in the pattern of the word "skip"? Show how you would do it.

4. Show how you might walk when you are feeling very *proud*.

5. Look at these words and choose one to act out just with body movements. The others in the class will try to guess which word you are acting out.

angry	busy	shy
silly	happy	discouraged
sad	fearful	excited

6. Make up a movement pattern that you can repeat over and over; for example, a hop, two skips, and a jump.

7. Pretend to be a zoo animal. Move about as that animal does. See if the others can guess the animal.

Activities on this page adapted with permission of the publisher from Betty Rowen's *Learning Through Movement*. (New York: Teachers College Press, copyright 1963 by Teachers College, Columbia University.)

6. Pretend you are fishing. Show by your movements some of the things a fisherman does.

7. You can walk fast and you can walk slowly. In what other ways can you walk? Be ready to show some ways.

8. Pretend you are bouncing a ball. Show how you would bounce it *low*. Then show how you would bounce it *high*.

9. Look at the picture of the seals, and read the poem about them. Then be ready to move about as the seals in the poem did.

The Seals

The seals all flap
Their shining flips
And bounce balls on
Their nosey tips,
And beat a drum,
And catch a bar,
And wriggle with
How pleased they are.

"The Seals" reprinted by permission of G. P. Putnam's Sons from *Hop, Skip and Jump* by Dorothy Aldis. Copyright 1934 by Dorothy Aldis; renewed 1961 by Dorothy Aldis.

Checking Up

Fill In the Missing Words

Copy sentences 1 to 5 on your paper and fill in the missing word or words. Do not write in this book.

1. The bending places in your skeleton are called j___.
2. The m___ that are fastened to your bones help you move about.
3. The trunk is the part of your body from your shoulders to the top of your l___.
4. A person who plays fair is a good sp___.
5. L___ movements help you move from one place to another.

Yes or No?

Write the numbers from 6 to 10 on a piece of paper. After each number, write the correct answer, *yes* or *no,* for each sentence.

6. A good sport takes turns.
7. A good sport does not make fun of others.
8. You can move from place to place in many different ways.
9. The muscles in your back are tiny and weak.
10. Good posture helps keep you from getting tired.

Number of Answers   10
Number Right   ___

5 What Foods Should You Eat?

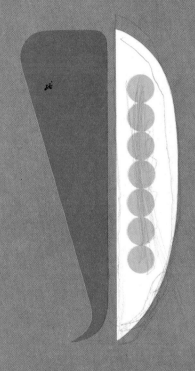

A Poem to Read About Vegetables

A carrot has a green fringed top;
    A beet is royal red;
And lettuces are curious
    All curled and run to head.

Some beans have strings to tie them on,
    And, what is still more queer,
Ripe corn is nothing more or less
    Than one enormous ear!

But when potatoes all have eyes,
    Why is it they should be
Put in the ground and covered up—
    Where it's too dark to see?

All Kinds of Vegetables

What vegetables does the poem on page 116 tell about?

Which of these vegetables do you eat at home?

What words does the poem use to tell about each vegetable? What do the pictures tell you?

You need to eat some vegetables every day. If you can, you should eat a dark-green vegetable or a deep-yellow vegetable every day—or at least three or four times a week. Remember to wash raw fruits and vegetables before you eat them.

Now look at the vegetables in the pictures on pages 118 and 119. See how many vegetables you can name.

Is a vegetable shown that you have eaten only a few times? If so, what is the vegetable? Did you like it? What are some other vegetables you have not yet eaten that you now think you would like to try?

How would you answer the question about vegetables on page 118?

Vegetables come in many forms. Some are fresh; some are canned. What other form do you see here?

There Are Many Ways to Serve Foods

You have probably noticed that there is more than one way of serving a vegetable. For example, the pictures below show some different ways of serving carrots. In which of these ways would the carrots be crunchy to eat? Which ways show differences in color?

How many different ways do you know of serving each of these vegetables: *corn, tomatoes, cabbage, potatoes, sweet potatoes, green beans?*

Carrot Pie

Shredded Carrot-and-Raisin Salad

Carrots and Peas

Raw Carrot Sticks

Baked Carrots

Carrot Sticks Dipped in Cream Cheese

Did you ever stop to think how many different ways there are of cooking and serving eggs?

Look at the pictures below to see some of these ways.

Which of these ways do you like eggs cooked and served?

Omelet

Boiled Eggs

Poached Egg on Toast

Egg-in-a-Hole

Scrambled Eggs

Fried Egg

What Is a Daily Food Guide?

There are four main groups of foods you should try to eat every day—or at least most days! You need all these foods to keep you healthy.

Vegetable-Fruit Group (4 or more servings)   Meat Group (2 or more servings)

122

The four main food groups are shown on these pages. How many servings do you need from each food group every day?

Milk Group (2 to 3 cups)   Bread-Cereal Group (4 or more servings)

How Can You Explore Foods?

Are any of the foods your family especially likes pictured on these two pages? What are some foods your family likes and wants to have often?

Different families have different favorites among foods. Often they have different ways of serving the same foods. Also families in one part of the country have foods not so well known in other parts.

It's fun to explore foods that are different from the ones you usually eat. Sometimes you do this when you eat at the home of a friend.

Blueberry Pie

Baked Beans with Brown Bread

Grits

Fried Cut Corn

Fried Chicken

Hot Dogs

Sometimes you learn about new foods in the school lunchroom. You may also try new foods in a restaurant or other eating place away from home.

You can explore foods sometimes, too, when you go to a summer camp or go somewhere on a vacation.

On pages 126 to 129, you will find a story about Kenny, who had a good chance to explore—in his own neighborhood—some foods prepared in ways that were new to him. Read to see what Kenny learned about foods, and about mothers, too.

Tortillas and Enchiladas

Bagels

Shish Kebab

Lobster

Spaghetti and Meat Sauce

Egg Rolls

What Did Kenny Learn About Foods and Mothers?

Once upon a very special day, Mother put an extra plate on the table. Kenny was bringing a friend home for lunch. He was Manuel Gomez, a new boy in Kenny's class.

Mother met the boys at the door. "Hello, Manuel," she said. "Welcome to our home! I am so glad you came."

What a wonderful lunch they had! There was cold tomato juice and there were big juicy hamburgers on buns. There were cookies and chocolate pudding and milk. How those boys ate!

Soon it was time to go back to school.

"Thank you, Mrs. Lee," said Manuel. "It was a very good lunch."

"I'm glad you enjoyed it, Manuel," said Mother. "I hope you come again soon."

A few days later, Kenny said to Mother,
"Manuel invited me to his house for lunch."

"That's nice," said Mother.

"But I don't want to go," said Kenny.

"Why not?" said Mother.

"His mother doesn't speak English,"
said Kenny.

"That doesn't matter," said Mother.
"Manuel will tell you what she says."

"They don't eat the same kind of food
we eat," said Kenny.

"I'm sure you will enjoy the lunch," said
Mother. "You should go, Kenny. Manuel
will feel sad if you don't."

So Kenny went to Manuel's house for
lunch.

Mrs. Gomez met the boys at the door. She smiled and said something Kenny did not understand. Manuel told him. It was "Hello, Kenny! You are welcome in our home. I am so happy that you came."

The boys looked at each other and laughed. "That was just what my mother said to you, Manuel," said Kenny.

What a wonderful lunch they had! There was bean soup; there was chicken with rice. There were baked bananas, cookies, and milk. How those boys ate!

Soon it was time to go back to school.

"Thank you, Mrs. Gomez," said Kenny. "That was a very good lunch!"

Again Mrs. Gomez said something that Kenny did not understand. Manuel told him. It was "I'm glad you liked the lunch. Please come again soon, Kenny."

The boys looked at each other and laughed. "That's just what your mother said to me, Kenny!" said Manuel.

When Kenny got home after school, he told his mother all about his lunch at the Gomez home.

"It is good to learn to eat different kinds of food," said Mother.

"Yes," said Kenny. "I didn't know before how much fun it could be to try new kinds of food."

"I learned something else, Mother," Kenny went on. "I learned that mothers are the same whether they speak English or not. They say the same kinds of things to us. And they know how to give good lunches to hungry boys!"

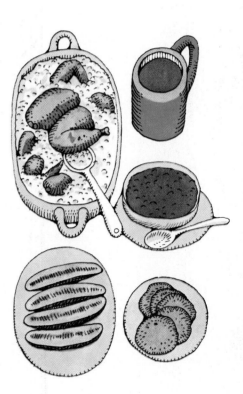

1. Tell about some different ways of serving bread.
2. Think of a food you once did not know about but now like. Tell how you learned to like it.
3. Think of a food you like to eat. Then write about it, as the boy did below. Tell why you like the food. Is it the food's color? Is it the taste? Do you like to chew it?

Why I Like Chicken

Chicken is a food I like. My mother makes it very crisp. My mother makes it real brown and it's very good when it's crisp. I like to hear it crunch when I eat it.

4. Many children in the world today do not get
   enough of the important foods they need. In
   many parts of the world things are being done
   to help children get the foods they need.
   For example, scientists have made a soft drink
   out of soybeans that is rich in food value.
   Watch the newspaper for pictures like the one
   shown below of children eating a new kind of
   food. See if you can find articles about new
   foods—such as fish flour—that are being made
   today. Be ready to tell about the articles.

Checking Up

Yes or No?

Copy the numbers from 1 to 10 on your paper. After each number write the correct answer, *yes* or *no,* for each sentence.

1. You should try to drink two or three cups of milk each day.
2. You can get some of the milk you need by eating such foods as cheese and ice cream.
3. One of the four important food groups is this: Soft Drinks and Candy.
4. You should try to eat a dark-green or deep-yellow vegetable at least three or four times a week.
5. All families eat foods cooked the same way.
6. There is more than one way to serve such foods as vegetables, fruits, milk drinks, and eggs.
7. We like foods only because they look pretty.
8. When you are served a food you have never eaten before, a good thing to do is taste it.
9. Eating enough of the right kinds of foods helps you keep healthy and well.
10. The four important food groups are *Milk, Vegetables and Fruits, Meat,* and *Breads and Cereals.*

Number of Answers   10

Number Right   ____

6 What Are Microbes?

133

What Do You Know About Microbes?

Did you know that there are tiny *microbes* all around you—in the air, in the ground, and in the water? They are small, but they are just as real and alive as you are, although in a different way.

Microbes can eat, grow, and get rid of wastes, just as people do. They can reproduce others like themselves. And like all living things, sooner or later they die.

Many of these microbes are tiny plants, or *bacteria*. Others are tiny animals. Of course they are quite different from the kinds of plants and animals you are used to seeing. You cannot see them because they are so small.

You can see a microbe only when it is put under a microscope that makes it look very large.

It may surprise you to learn that many, if not most, microbes are helpful and not harmful. Some helpful microbes are those that make changes in soil so that plants will grow well in it. Other helpful microbes are used to make medicines. Still others are used as "helpers" to make such foods as bread, pickles, and cheese.

The harmful microbes are the *disease germs* that make people sick. Other harmful ones are the kinds that get into food and cause it to spoil.

What Are Bacteria?

Microbes that are likely to be in your house at all
times are the ones known as *bacteria.* There are many
kinds of bacteria. But if you looked at them under
a microscope, as the scientist is doing here, you
would see that they have just three main shapes.

Look at the pictures on page 137.
What are the three main shapes of bacteria?

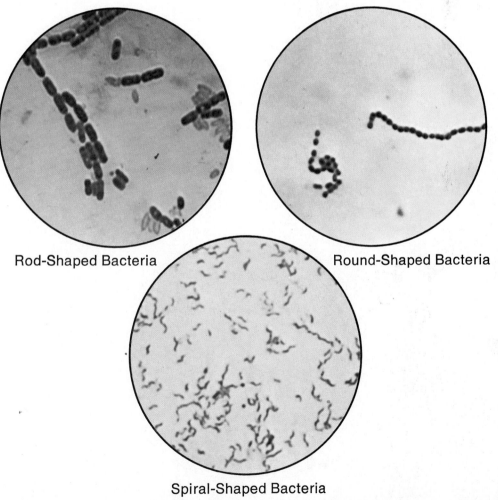

Rod-Shaped Bacteria

Round-Shaped Bacteria

Spiral-Shaped Bacteria

How Do Bacteria Grow?

When bacteria reach a certain size, they divide or split in two. Each one doubles itself. One tiny plant becomes two, two become four, four become eight, eight become sixteen, and so on. From a single one of the bacteria it is possible for millions of bacteria to grow in just 48 hours!

Some bacteria grow *alone;* others grow in *pairs;* still others grow in *chains.* Bacteria may also grow in different kinds of *clumps* or in *threads.* Look at the pictures below and on page 139 to see these different ways in which bacteria grow.

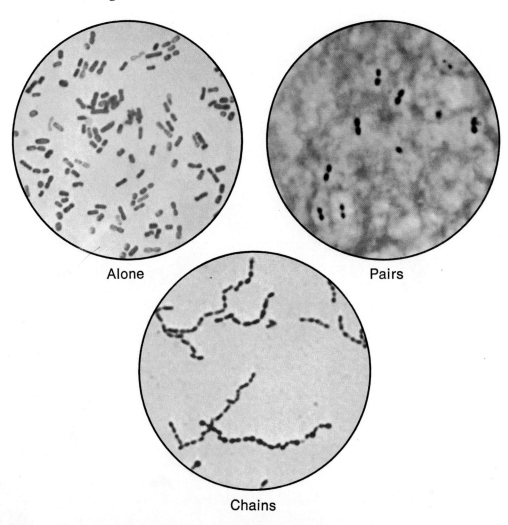

Alone

Pairs

Chains

Bacteria grow best in wet places, in dark places, and in warm places. Most bacteria can be killed by dryness, by sunlight, or by very high temperatures. When milk is *pasteurized,* a high temperature is used to get rid of harmful germs. The milk is first heated to a very high temperature. Then it is cooled and stored in a cold place. Do you know why?

Most bacteria stop growing, or grow very slowly, in a cold or very low temperature. This is why milk, after it is pasteurized, is kept in a cold place.

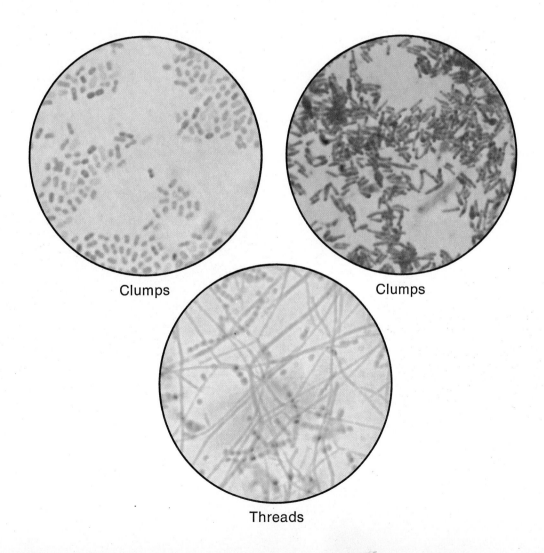

Clumps

Clumps

Threads

What Are Viruses?

You may have heard something about another kind of microbe. This is the tiniest microbe of all. It is known as a *virus*. Viruses are so tiny they can be seen only with a very powerful *electron microscope,* like the one shown here.

Scientists have learned some things about viruses, but there is much yet to be discovered. For example, scientists have had trouble deciding whether viruses are tiny plants or tiny animals.

All the viruses we know about today are harmful ones. These harmful viruses cause such diseases as chicken pox, flu, polio, mumps, measles, and colds.

Has the doctor given you shots to protect you against any of these diseases?

Below you can see some viruses as they would look when viewed through an electron microscope. These viruses are enlarged thousands of times. What diseases are caused by the three shown below?

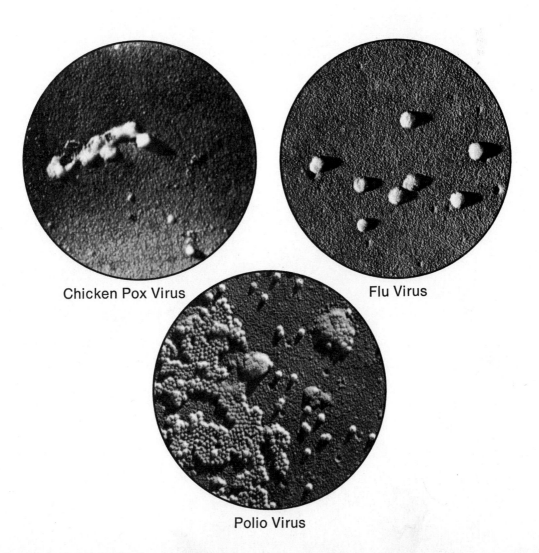

Chicken Pox Virus

Flu Virus

Polio Virus

What Are Molds?

Another kind of microbe almost sure to be found in your house are the tiny plants called *molds.* You have seen bread with greenish or blackish mold on it.

Molds like those on bread grow very fast. Bread mold starts as one tiny spot. Next the mold grows to a white thread, which grows longer and branches out many times. Soon there is a great tangle of white threads. Some of the threads grow straight up, and little black balls, or *spores,* appear at the ends of the threads. Look at the pictures below to see how bread mold grows.

Mold starts as a tiny spot.

White threads branch out.

Mold spores as seen under a microscope.

Molds grow best where there is some dampness.

Some molds are helpful and are used to make certain kinds of cheese taste good. Can you find a helpful cheese mold below?

Some molds spoil food. Below you can see some spoiled fruit with spots of fuzzy, brownish mold on it.

Scientists also use molds in making medicines called *antibiotics*. *Penicillin* is one of these antibiotics. Can you find a penicillin mold below?

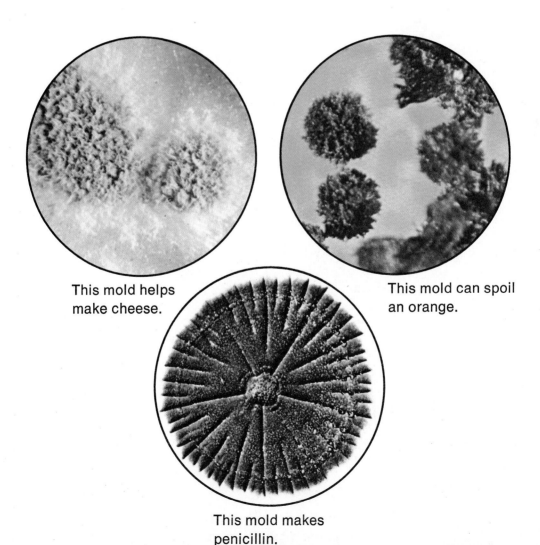

This mold helps make cheese.

This mold can spoil an orange.

This mold makes penicillin.

How Do You Keep Healthy?

Perhaps you wonder how you can stay healthy most of the time since microbes are all around you and since some of these microbes can cause disease. You stay healthy partly because your body has ways of fighting off harmful microbes.

For example, most of the germs that come into your body with the food you eat are killed by the juices in your stomach. If harmful microbes should get into your lungs, they are likely to be coughed up.

If disease germs get into your body through a cut, there are certain cells in your blood—*white blood cells*—that travel to the cut and kill some of the germs. These white blood cells also form a wall around germs and keep them from spreading further in the body. See the pictures on page 145 of a white blood cell "eating up" a disease germ.

There are things you can remember to do every day that will help protect you and others from harmful microbes. You can see some of these things pictured on pages 146 and 147. What are they?

Below you can see a large white blood cell swallowing up a rod-shaped disease germ. You can see how long it took the white cell to completely surround, or "eat up," the disease germ. How many seconds did it take? Look at the bottom right picture to find out.

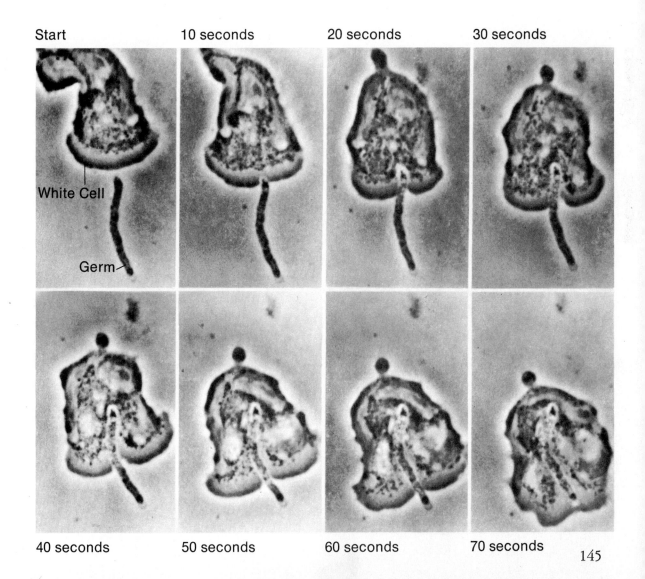

Start   10 seconds   20 seconds   30 seconds

White Cell

Germ

40 seconds   50 seconds   60 seconds   70 seconds

Cover your coughs and sneezes with a tissue or handkerchief so you will not spread germs of colds or other diseases.

Wash your hands before you eat or handle food and after you use the toilet. Soap and warm water can wash away harmful microbes that may be on your hands.

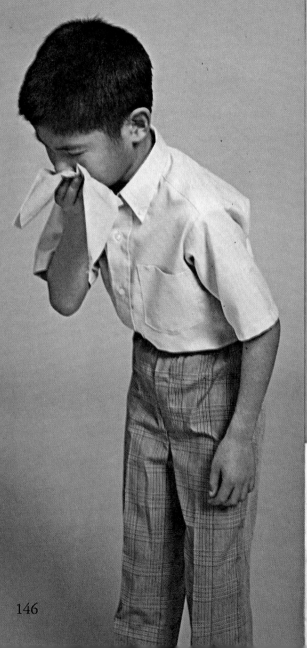

146

Use your *own* towel and washcloth.
Do you know why?

Keep pencils and other objects out of
your mouth. And keep fingers out, too!

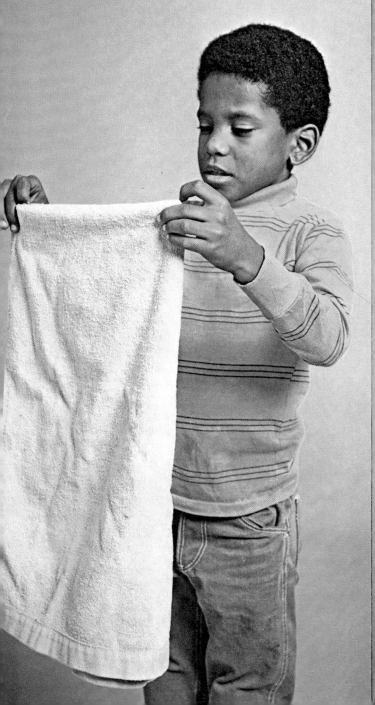

Things to Think About

1. Why do you not put dried foods such as flour and rice in the refrigerator or freezer?
2. Why do you think you are told not to rub your eyes with your fingers?
3. Why does the dentist wash his hands before he examines your teeth?
4. What would you have to do if you wanted to see a virus?
5. Your body has many interesting ways of protecting itself from harmful microbes. What are some of these ways?
6. Why is it important to wash your hands before you eat?
7. Why is milk at the dairy pasteurized?

Things to Do

1. Here is something you can do at school or at home to see how microbes from the air settle on foods and grow.

   Put a slice of banana, a slice of apple, and a slice of cooked potato on a small dish.

   Let the food stand in the open air for an hour or so.

   Cover the dish with a piece of aluminum foil. Put the dish in a warm, dark place.

   Uncover the dish to look at the food every day. In two or three days you will see some groups of microbes. Some may be smooth and shiny. Others may be fuzzy, threadlike molds. If there is a magnifying glass in your classroom, look at the microbes through it.

2. If you want to learn more about microbes, look for these books at the library: *The True Book of Bacteria* by Anne Frahm (Childrens Press) and *Microbes at Work* by Millicent Selsam (Morrow).

More Things to Do

1. Here is one good way to watch a mold grow.

   Moisten a slice of bread.

   Put it on a small plate and let it stand in the open air for an hour.

   Cover the plate with aluminum foil.

   Look at the slice of bread every day—with a magnifying glass if possible.

   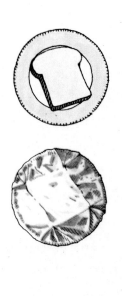

   Watch for the white, threadlike mold that appears first and then for the little black balls containing spores.

2. If you want to see how cold temperatures slow down the growth of microbes, here is something you can do at home.

   Put two slices of moistened bread on two plates, and let them stand in the open air for an hour or so.

   Then cover each plate with aluminum foil. Put one plate of moist bread in the refrigerator, and put the other one in a warm place.

   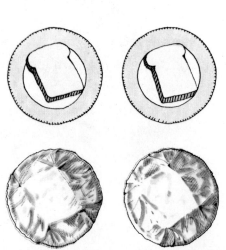

   Look at the two slices of bread every day. Notice how each one looks after three or four days.

3. Look around your kitchen at home and see what foods you can find that are kept from spoiling because they are dried. Maybe you already know some of these foods. What are some of them?

4. There is something you can do to show that microbes need moisture to grow.

   Put some dry beans in one small glass.
   Put several spoonfuls of flour in another.

   Put some dry beans and enough water to cover them in a third glass.

   Put some flour and enough water to cover it in a fourth glass. Put the flour in the glass first.

   Watch the glasses for three or four days. Find out which foods begin to spoil—the dry ones or the ones in water. You will know the spoiled food by its sour smell.

Special Research

See if you can find out how the pioneers in our country kept foods from spoiling in the days when there were no refrigerators. One book you might read is *The True Book of Pioneers* by Mabel Harmer (Childrens Press).

Checking Up

Yes or No?

Write the numbers from 1 to 10 on your paper. After each number write the correct answer, *yes* or *no,* for each sentence.

1. Microbes are tiny living plants and animals.
2. Microbes are found only in dirty places.
3. There are microbes on your hands and on your clothes.
4. All microbes are harmful.
5. When a food spoils, it is likely that microbes have been at work in it.
6. Scientists use some molds in making medicines known as antibiotics.
7. Molds can be helpful to us.
8. It takes a very powerful microscope to help you see a virus.
9. Millions of bacteria can grow from just one microbe in two days' time or less.
10. Bacteria grow in very high temperatures.

Fill In the Missing Words

Copy sentences 11 to 15 on your paper and fill in the missing word or words. Do not write in this book.

11. Some harmful kinds of microbes are disease g___.
12. Mumps and flu are caused by v___.
13. Bacteria grow best in dark places, in places that are not too cold, and in w___ places.
14. Bacteria grow by d___.
15. Some microbes are tiny animals and some are tiny p___.

Number of Answers   15

Number Right   ___

7 How Does a Community Work for Health?

How Does a Community Keep Healthy?

There are many things you and your family can do
to keep yourselves healthy. You know what some
of these things are, don't you? What are they?

Sometimes you need the help of others in staying
healthy, or in getting well if you are sick. There are
health workers in the community who can give
you and your family this help. Some of these workers
are shown above and on page 155. Do you know
who they are? What do you think they do?

Often in a community there is also a special city
or county health department which checks to make
sure that important health work is carried on to
protect people from disease.

One kind of health worker that you may know about is the public health nurse. Can you find her at the far left on page 154? She goes into homes where there are health problems and tries to help solve the problems. Other health workers make sure that the food you eat is safe and that the water and milk you drink are clean and pure.

Still other workers help keep streets and alleys clean. Or they may help solve problems of dirty air, or *air pollution*. How do you think they do this?

One pages 156 to 171 you will read about some of these community health workers. You will find out what they do to help keep you healthy.

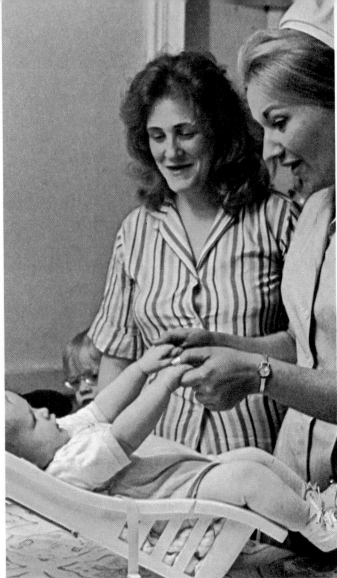

What Does a Public Health Nurse Do?

Public health nurses work mainly with families in the community. Sometimes these nurses also work in schools in a community. When a public health nurse goes into a home, she shows a family things they can do to stay healthy. In the pictures on this page and on page 157 you can see a public health nurse during a day's work. Read to find out some things she does.

Page 156. Left. *A public health nurse starts her day's work.*
Right. *She goes to visit a home where there is a new baby, and she shows the mother how to take care of the baby.*

This page. Left. *She explains about use of eyeglasses to a young child who has just been fitted for them.*
Right. *Later, when the nurse gets back to her office, she makes a record of her day's visits for future use.*

How Are Milk and Meat Kept Safe?

The health workers on this page and page 159
are helping make sure that the milk you drink and
the meat you eat are clean and pure. Read page 159
to find out how they are doing this.

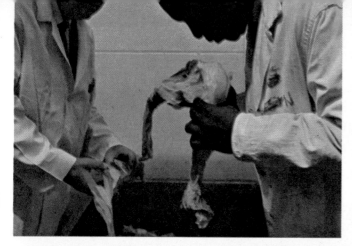

Page 158. Top left. *At a dairy, an inspector tests a milk sample to be sure that harmful bacteria have been killed.*
Top right. *An inspector is checking the temperature of milk in a storage tank. Why must the milk be kept cold?*
Bottom. *Automatic machines fill and seal cartons of milk. An inspector then checks the cartons before they are packed.*

This page. Top left. *At a meat plant, the food inspector looks carefully at chickens to make sure that there are no signs of disease.*
Top right. *Workers called* sanitarians *check the temperature of meat that is being ground to make sure that it is cold enough for safety.*
Bottom: *Sausages are checked to see if they are made in safe ways.*

How Is Water Made Safe to Drink?

The drinking water in the community must be kept safe to drink. To make sure it is safe, water that is taken from a river or lake or public well is piped first to a *water-treatment plant*. Here it is treated to make it pure and safe to drink. Next it goes through large pipes, or *tunnels*, to pumping stations. Then it is pumped through pipes to homes. Read to learn what happens at the water-treatment plant.

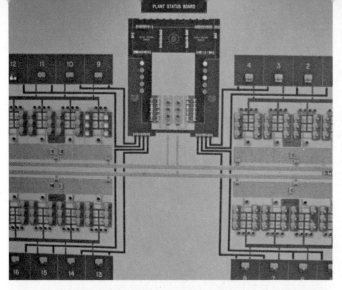

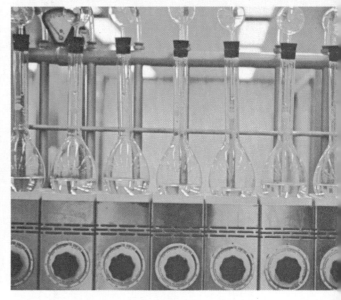

Page 160. *View from the air of Chicago's water-treatment plant. This plant treats, filters, and thus purifies more than a million gallons of water per minute.* This page. Top left. *On this control panel, engineers can check what is happening in any part of the water-treatment plant.*

Top right. *After water is pumped into the plant, chemicals are mixed into the water. The water then flows to* settling basins, *and impurities begin to settle out.* Bottom left. *Next, the water goes into tanks that have layers of sand and gravel, which filter out dirt and solids.* Bottom right. *In the plant laboratory, water samples are tested for safety.*

How Is Sewage Treated?

Household wastes, or *sewage,* must be got rid of in safe ways. Many communities have *sewage-treatment plants* for this purpose. Sewage is brought to a plant—through sewers from pipes in the home—and is treated to make it pure enough to empty into rivers or lakes. This treatment keeps the rivers and lakes from becoming *polluted.* What can you learn about a sewage-treatment plant from these pictures?

Page 162. *View from the air of a sewage-treatment plant. When sewage reaches the plant, various things are done to it to settle out heavy particles, to kill harmful bacteria, and to help remove unpleasant odors.*

This page. Top left. *Here you can see a new underground sewer being constructed. It will carry wastes, or sewage, to the plant.*

Top right. *In these* settling tanks, *heavy particles settle to the bottom. The settled material is called* sludge.

Bottom left. *From the settling tanks, water goes into final treatment tanks. Here air is added, among other things, for further purifying.*

Bottom right. *Finally the sewage is pure enough to be emptied into a nearby river or lake.*

What Can Be Done About Dirty Air?

Another problem many communities face today is that of keeping the air clean. More and more, communities are trying hard to keep the air from becoming dirty. This is important because dirty air that is breathed into the lungs can cause illness.

The picture on these two pages is a photograph
taken in a city in broad daylight, though it seems
to have been taken at night or at twilight. Why is
the air in a city more likely to be polluted than air
in the country? What does this picture tell you about
why city air is often impure?

On pages 166 and 167 you can see some steps that
are being taken today to fight air pollution.

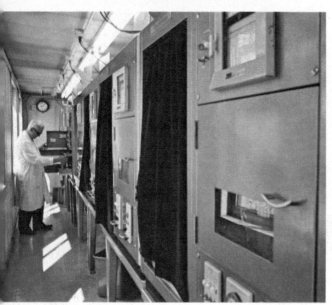

This page. Top left. *A jar covered with a sticky tape is placed on the top of this grey box. The sticky tape catches the dirty material in the air. Later, examination will show the type of dirt that can be found in the air and also the direction from which the material came.*

Top right. *At the laboratory, a filter is weighed to measure how much dirt and other harmful substances are in it.*

Bottom left. *At a checking station, a specially trained worker is inside studying machines that tell about harmful gases which are in the air outside.*

Bottom right. *Air samples are tested at the air-pollution control laboratory.*

This page. Top left. *A jar filled with water is left outside for a month, then removed. From the dirt that has settled at the bottom, scientists can find out the amount of dirt that falls out of the air in a square mile.*

Top right. *On this rack, metals of various kinds are placed. When the metals are studied at the laboratory, scientists can tell how dirty air may change the metals.*

Bottom left. *A revolving television camera, mounted on a rooftop, watches over the city. The picture is received on a television set in a control room. If a factory breaks the rules and sends harmful substances into the air, the camera can locate the source.*

Bottom right. *If a factory is found by the camera to be polluting the air, an investigator is sent to the factory.*

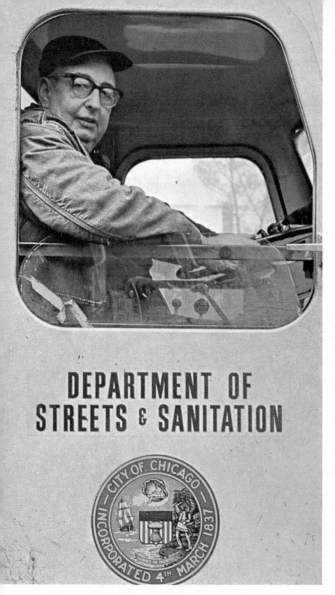

How Are Streets and Alleys Cleaned?

In a healthful community, it is important to have clean streets and alleys. This means that trash must be collected and disposed of in sanitary ways. Study the pictures on this page and page 169 to learn how these jobs are done in one community.

Page 168. Left. *A driver begins his workday with the big machine that sweeps up papers and trash.*
Right. *Round brooms and water-sprays in the machine help keep the streets clean and free of trash.*

This page. Top. *Men collect trash and junk that nobody wants.*
Bottom left. *Garbage of all kinds is loaded into the back of the truck.*
Bottom right. *Then the garbage-collecting machine chews and grinds the garbage into small pieces and pushes it into the truck.*

How Can We Get Rid of Garbage?

Once the garbage has been collected, there is a problem of getting rid of it in sanitary ways. Some communities burn the garbage after it has been collected. This method may not be used in years to come, though, since it may add to air pollution, if care is not taken. Other communities bury their garbage. In the pictures here you can see what happens to garbage that is burned.

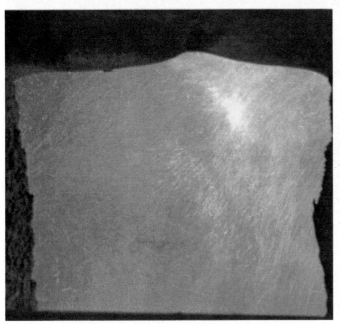

Page 170. *Garbage trucks empty their contents onto the floor of the incinerator building. Here the garbage is first sprayed to reduce dust from dumping. Then it is picked up by huge cranes, carried over the wall, and dropped into the incinerator for burning.*

This page. Top left. *Before the garbage trucks enter the incinerator building, each one is weighed.*

Top right. *A man checks the burning garbage in the incinerator. This garbage-burning plant has special equipment to avoid polluting the air.*

Bottom left. *Heat in the incinerator reaches a red-hot temperature.*

Bottom right. *The garbage that does not burn, such as tin cans, is carried up a conveyor belt to be dumped into another truck and taken away to be buried.*

Things to Do

1. Did you know that there are many kinds of nurses? There are school nurses, public health nurses, hospital nurses, nurses for the army and navy, nurses in factories, and many other kinds, too. If you want to learn more about these nurses, look for a book about nurses in the school or public library.

2. Write a story telling what you have learned about the work of public health nurses.

3. Tell about some things a doctor can do to keep you healthy—things you cannot do for yourself.

4. See if you can find out what your community does with garbage after it is collected.

5. Find out if your community has these places and, if so, where they are located: *health department office, water-treatment plant, sewage-treatment plant.*

6. The next time you go into a food store or restaurant in your community, look to see if there is a sign showing that it has been inspected by the health department.

7. Your community does many things to help keep you *safe* as well as to help keep you healthy. Tell what safety aids you see in the pictures below. Then tell about some safety aids in *your* community. Tell why these aids are needed. Think, too, of other places where signs might be needed.

Checking Up

Fill In the Missing Words

Copy sentences 1 to 5 on your paper and fill in the missing word or words. Do not write in this book.

1. Public health nurses spend most of their time working with f___ in the community.
2. Sometimes you and your family need help from others in staying h___ or in getting well if you have been s___.
3. One of the public health workers you know about is the public health n___.
4. In a community there is sometimes a h___ d___ that helps protect the health of everyone.
5. It is important that people in a community have pure, safe w___ to drink and pure a___ to br___.

Yes or No?

Write the numbers from 6 to 10 on your paper. After each number write the correct answer, *yes* or *no,* for each sentence.

6. Do some communities bury their garbage?
7. Is *polluted* air dirty air?
8. Are there household wastes in sewage?
9. Does sanitary mean "not clean"?
10. Does a community need to take care of its garbage?

Number of Answers   10
Number Right   ____

8 In How Many Ways Can You Grow?

A Poem About Growing Tall

"How tall?" they say.
"You're taller!" they cry.
He stands in the hall
to measure his tall
new tallness.

       All
they do is to lay
a book on his head
so it's good and square
by the door-jamb where
old pencil marks compare.

Such talk, such bustle!
"Don't *lean* on the door,
Don't move a muscle!"
He doesn't.
He thought that he was taller before.
He wasn't.

How Do You Grow?

Maybe you, too, find it exciting to get measured now and then to see how much you have grown.

At times, though, you may have some questions about how you or your friends are growing. You may wonder why it is that your friends—especially those who are the same age as you—aren't the same size as you. And you may wonder why some children are much bigger than others the same age.

If you wonder about such things, you need to remember that every person is different from every other one. And each person has a different way of growing. You will grow *your* way, and other boys and girls your age will grow *their* way.

Soon now some of you may start to grow very fast. But others of you may wait for some years before you begin your rapid growing.

Each of you has your own way of growing.
And if you get enough sleep and outdoor exercise
and enough of the right kinds of foods, you will
grow in the way that is right for *you*.

All are eight-year-olds. All are strong and well.

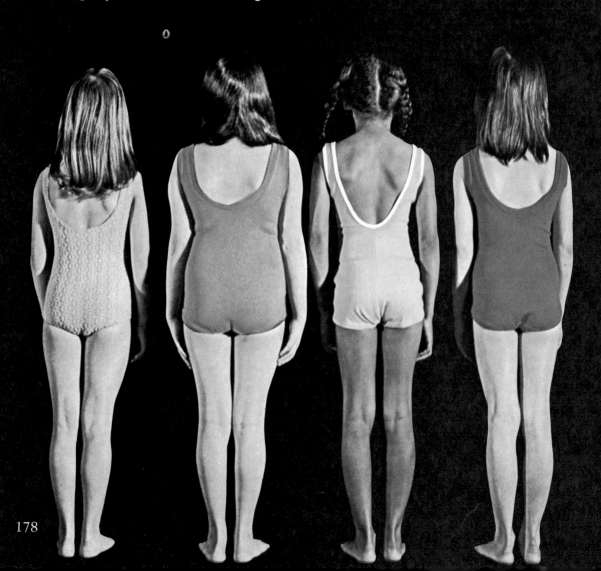

Study the pictures on these two pages.

What can you learn from looking at the pictures of the girls on page 178.

What do you notice in the pictures of the boys on this page?

But each one grows in a different way.

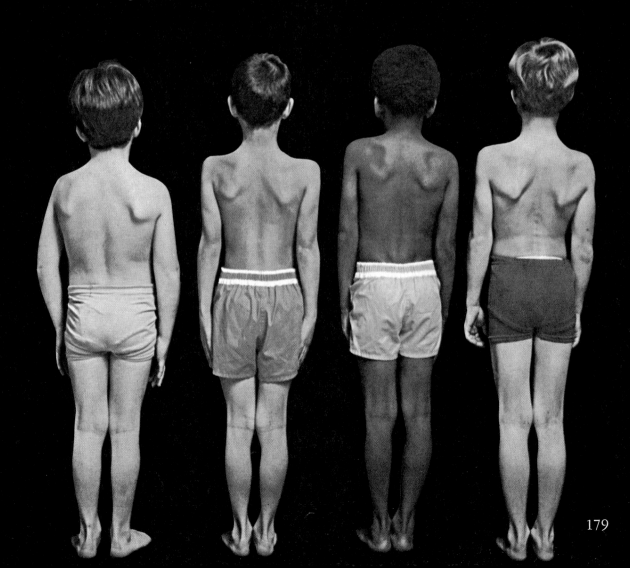

179

How Is Each Human Baby Different?

From the time you were a baby, you have had your own way of growing. For example, you may have started to talk before other babies your age; but others may have started to walk before you did.

Even though all babies have their own way of growing—and each one is different from every other baby—in certain ways they are alike in the way they grow. All babies grow rapidly in the first year. Study the pictures on these two pages.

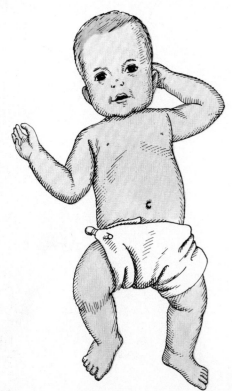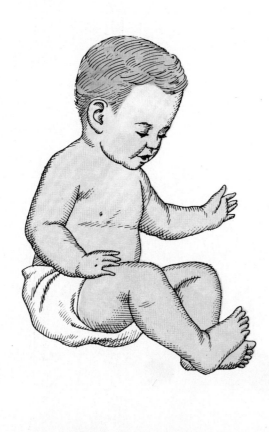

In these pictures, you can see a baby at different times during the first year of life. The baby has learned to move about and sit up and crawl. But even at one year of age, he is just beginning to stand alone. He is just beginning to learn to walk and talk. He could not live without care from others.

That is why families are so important to human babies. Families are important to children during all the rest of the growing-up years, too. Why?

How Do Babies Grow?

All animal and human babies grow before they are born as well as after. Some animal babies such as chickens, birds, turtles, and snakes grow in eggs—outside the mother's body—before they are hatched. Here you can see a baby chick, a baby bird, a baby turtle, and a baby snake—each one just beginning to be hatched from an egg.

Human babies, and the babies of many animals, such as dogs, hippopotamuses, bears, and foxes, grow inside the mother's body before they are born.

How Do Animal Babies Grow Up?

One answer to the question above can be found in the pictures and captions on this page. What interesting information can you find out?

A puppy will become a full-grown dog in about a year.

A baby hippopotamus will reach its full size within one year.

A baby bear will be almost full-grown in two years.

A baby fox will be grown-up by the time it is about five months old. 183

Are There Other Ways to Grow?

You have been reading mostly about *physical* growth, that is about growing in weight and height. But weighing more and growing tall are not the only ways to grow. Another way to grow is in being able to handle your feelings, or *emotions.* You can learn ways of handling them that help you and that do not hurt others.

Little children often cry when they are angry or otherwise upset. Or they may hit at others. But older children, like you, can grow in finding better ways to handle your upset feelings.

Let's stop and see how much you know about ways of handling upset feelings.

Look at Andy, pictured on page 185, who is angry. What is making him feel that way? What do you think Andy might do to get over his angry feelings?

Now look at Susan, also pictured on page 185. Susan is feeling scared and shy. What is making her feel that way? What do you think she should do?

Now turn to pages 186 and 187 to find out about some helpful ways to handle angry feelings and scared or shy feelings.

Mother: "Andy, I know how you feel because your toy is broken. But you cannot hit little Billy! Next time, let's be sure your things are put away."

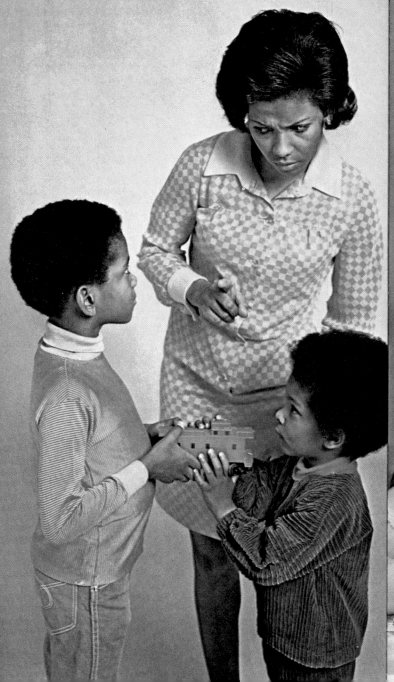

Susan: "I'm supposed to give a report at school this morning. I *want* to do it but I'm scared. Maybe I should say I'm not ready yet. Oh, dear! What should I do?"

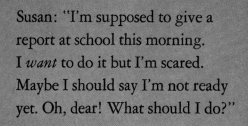

185

What Can You Do About Angry Feelings?

Andy, whom you saw on page 185, had a right to
be angry, didn't he? We all feel angry when
something we own has been broken. Sometimes,
too, we feel angry when we think we have been
treated unfairly or left out of things. And at times it
is hard to get over our angry feelings.

What can you do about angry feelings that stay
with you for a while? Instead of hitting or hurting
others, try talking things over. Andy, for example,
might talk over with his mother or father what he,
Andy, can do to keep Billy from getting into his
things.

Talking over your angry feelings with your parents
or with someone else you trust is better for you than
keeping your feelings locked up inside you. For as
long as the angry feelings are inside you, you will
feel mean and unhappy.

If there is nobody around to talk with about your
angry feelings, try to turn to something else for
a while. Take a walk, ride your bike, play a game, or
watch an interesting program on TV. Doing such
things will help until you have a chance to talk out
your feelings.

What Can You Do When You Are Afraid?

Susan, whom you saw on page 185, had mixed feelings, didn't she? She wanted to give her report to the class, and yet she didn't want to because she felt a little scared.

What Susan should know is that everybody has feelings like these at times. The feelings often come with learning to do new things or trying to do things you think you can't do very well.

What can you do about scared feelings? First of all, remember that you are not the only one who feels that way now and then.

Sometimes it helps to talk over your scared or shy feelings with your mother or father, your teacher, or some other person you trust.

Most of the time, it helps if you can go ahead and try the things you are afraid of doing. Many times the feelings soon go away. Susan, for example, might find that her scared feelings would disappear once she got started with her report.

Of course there are times when you really should be scared, such as being afraid to take a foolish dare. Then being afraid can keep you or others safe.

Can you think of a time when *you* felt scared or shy? What did you do? What would you do now?

How Can You Grow As a Family Member?

Another way in which you can grow is in being a good family member. Now that you are eight years old or more, you will find that there are many ways you can help share the work at home. Some of these ways are shown below and on page 189. What are they?

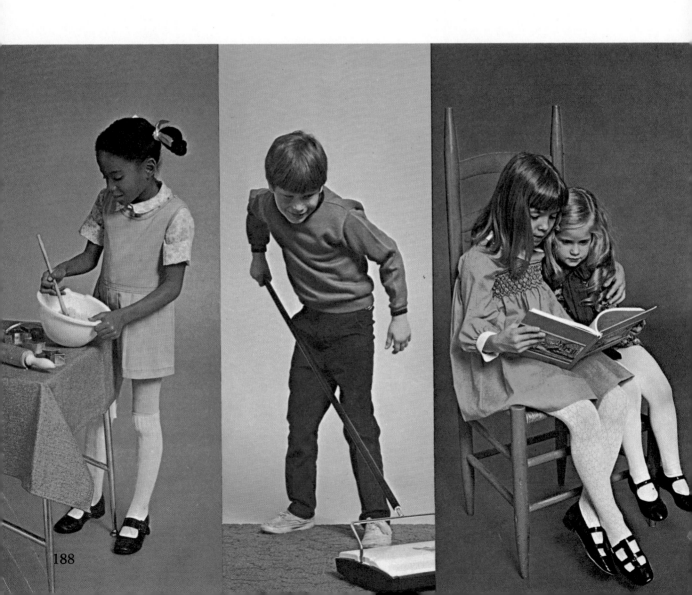

You can be sure you are improving in being a good family member if you help at home in ways like these and if you do not have to be reminded all the time to do these things.

How do *you* help at home? What do you do now that you couldn't do when you were younger?

Can You Grow in Making Decisions?

Still another way in which you can grow is in doing what your best judgment tells you to do—no matter what others are doing.

Sometimes you may have a problem like Dick, the boy in the story "Should I or Shouldn't I?" shown below. Read the story, then be ready to tell about Dick's problem.

Should I or Shouldn't I?

Dick Banta had a hard time when his family first moved to a new neighborhood.

Not many boys lived in Dick's apartment building, and the boys in his new school all seemed to have their own friends. Dick missed his old friends, and he missed having someone to play with after school.

Sometimes Dick would stand around on the playground after school and watch the boys play ball. Now and then the boys would ask him to play ball with them.

One afternoon when Dick went out to the playground the boys were not playing ball. They were teasing some little boys and taking their caps away from them.

"Come on, Dick," called Pete. "See if *you* can get a cap."

"You're going to give the caps back, aren't you?" asked Dick.

"Maybe," replied Pete. "And maybe not."

"Oh," thought Dick. "I don't really want to do that. But the others are doing it. Should I or shouldn't I?"

Did you decide what Dick's problem was?

Was he worried about doing something just because the others were doing it, although *he* himself really didn't want to do it?

Or was he afraid that the boys he wanted for friends wouldn't like him if he didn't do what they were doing?

Or do you think his problem might be a little of both things?

What do you think Dick should do about his problem?

Now turn to page 192 and compare your answer with the ideas some other children and their teacher had.

Be ready to tell, too, about a time lately when you had a hard decision to make.

What was the decision? What did you do about it? Would you do something different if you had another chance?

"Dick might say, 'Oh, let's play ball. That is more fun!' Then the other boys might stop teasing the little guys and play ball."

Lee

"Dick might tell the boys he can't play and then go on home. That way, he wouldn't have to do something he thinks isn't right."

Nora

"If the older boys don't stop teasing, Dick might do something that is not easy to do. He might say, 'Let's be good sports and let the little boys alone. And let's give them back their caps.'

"Dick's problem is one we all have at times. Should we just go along with the others? Should we do what the others are doing for fear they won't like us if we don't? Or should we take a stand for what we think is right? What we decide to do depends on how grown-up we are as a person."

Mrs. Fernandaz

What Are Your Questions About Growing?

So far you have learned some interesting things about growing—both about physical growth and about growth as a person. What have you learned that you did not know before?

There may be other things about growing that you would like to know, too. Below are some questions that boys and girls your age have asked. How would you answer these questions?

Check your answers with the information given on the next page.

---

1. When does the brain stop growing?

---

2. Are there some parts of the body that never stop growing?

---

3. When do children stop growing tall?

What are some questions about growing that *you* have? How might you find answers to your questions?

Some Answers to Often-Asked Questions

When does the brain stop growing?

The brain grows fast during the early years of life, and it reaches almost its full size by the time a child is five years old. A little more growth takes place very slowly until a person is twenty or so. At its full size, the brain weighs about two and a half to three pounds.

But though the brain itself stops growing, a person can keep growing in the ability to put the brain to use. He or she can grow in knowing how to find out things, in knowing how to do things, and in knowing how to help take care of the body.

Are there some parts of the body that never stop growing?

Yes, there are. The skin, for example, grows all your lifetime. You shed dead cells from your skin each day. Your skin makes millions of new cells daily to take the place of the dead ones that are shed.

Your hair and nails keep on growing all your life, too. Your hair, for example, grows about half an inch each month or about five to six inches each year.

When do children stop growing tall?

Girls keep on growing in height until they are about sixteen or eighteen or so. Boys keep on growing until they are eighteen or twenty years old or thereabouts. After that, people may grow fatter but they will not grow taller.

Things to Do

1. You might make a record about yourself called *How I Grow,* as the chart at the right. Include shoe size, clothing size, height, and weight. Note the changes in size over periods of a few months.

	Sept.	Jan.	May

2. Listed below are some other ways you can grow. Be ready to tell or write about how you have grown in some of these ways in the past year or so. Many Ways to Grow:

   You can grow in being more *polite.*

   You can grow in being a *good sport.*

   You can grow in *learning new skills* such as using a dictionary or playing a musical instrument.

   You can grow in your ability *to take care of yourself*—to remember to bathe, brush your teeth, and shampoo your hair, for example.

3. Suppose a friend has made you very angry. You can't seem to get over your angry feelings. Be ready to act out what you might do about your angry feelings.

Checking Up

Yes or No?

Write the numbers from 1 to 10 on a piece of paper. After each number write the correct answer, *yes* or *no,* for each sentence.

1. Do all children the same age grow in exactly the same way?
2. Should all children the same age weigh the same?
3. Do all people sometimes feel angry?
4. Is growing taller and heavier the only way there is of growing?
5. Is hitting someone who makes you angry the best way to handle feelings of anger?
6. Is it usually helpful to go ahead, if you can, and do the thing you feel scared or shy about doing?
7. Is a good family member one who sits back and lets others do all the work?
8. Can you grow in learning to take care of yourself?
9. Should you always do just what the others you are with are doing?
10. Does it help when you have angry or scared or shy feelings to talk things over with your parents, your teacher, or some other grown-up?

Number of Answers   10

Number Right   ____

Self-Help Review of Book

Part 1: Do You Know?

See if you can answer each question below. If you cannot answer a question, look up the answer on the page or pages given after the question.

1. What do we mean by *posture?* What things can you do to improve your posture? (Pages 106 and 107)
2. Why should you take good care of your teeth? (Page 86)
3. About how many hours of sleep do you need each night? (Pages 34 and 35)
4. What are some good guides for TV-viewing? (Page 36)
5. Why should you eat foods from the four main food groups every day? (Pages 122 and 123)
6. In what kinds of places do bacteria grow best? (Page 138)
7. Why should you wash your hands before you eat and after using the toilet? (Page 146)
8. Why should you cover your coughs and sneezes? (Page 146)
9. Why are community health workers needed? (Page 154)
10. What are some things a public health nurse may do to help families? (Pages 156 and 157)
11. What can you do to help yourself get over angry, scared, or shy feelings? (Pages 184 to 187)

Part 2: What Are the Safe Things to Do?

See if you can answer each question below. If you cannot answer the question, look up the answer on the page or pages you see after the question.

1. How should you plug in or unplug a toaster? (Pages 58 to 60)

2. What are some guides for keeping safe when you are playing running games? (Pages 62 to 64)

3. What should you do if you have to reach for something in a high place? (Pages 50 to 52)

4. What checks should you make to see if a bicycle is safe to ride? (Pages 44 to 46)

5. What signal should you give if you are driving a bicycle and you want to make a left turn? A right turn? A stop? (Pages 48 to 50)

6. What safety rules should you follow when you are using playground equipment? (Pages 60 to 62)

7. What are some safe things to do during a fire drill at school? (Pages 52 to 54)

8. Do you always have to take a dare? What kinds of dares are unsafe? (Pages 66 to 68)

9. What are some ways to keep safe when you are in or around water? (Pages 54 to 56)

10. What are some signs that can help you keep safe? (Pages 56 to 58)

End-of-Book Test

Part 1: Fill In the Missing Words
Copy each sentence on a piece of
paper. Fill in the missing word or words
needed to make each sentence correct.
Do not write in this book.

1. A good time to brush the teeth is
   __ we eat.
2. Both food and sleep can give us
   __ for work and play.
3. We need our teeth to __ food and
   help make the food easier to digest.
4. The two main parts of a tooth are the
   __ and the __.
5. If we can't brush our teeth after we
   eat, we should be sure to brush them
   well at least __ a day.
6. The places in your body where two
   bones come together are called __.
7. The __ that are fastened to our
   bones help us move about.
8. The four important food groups
   in the daily food guide are
   __-__; __; __; and __-__.
9. Tiny plants and animals that are
   found in the world all around us and
   that can be seen only under a
   microscope are called __.
10. An important health problem that
    many communities face is keeping
    the air from getting __.

Number of Answers   10

Number Right   ____

Part 2: What Is It?

Copy each number from 1 to 10 on a piece of paper. After the number write the letter that stands for the body part described. For example, 1, g.

1. Parts of the body that help us make strong motions.
2. Tiny tubes that carry blood through the body.
3. Juice in the mouth that starts to digest food.
4. The voice box.
5. The part of the body that acts on messages received from the senses.
6. Parts of the body that always have air in them.
7. A part of the air you must have to live.
8. A large gland that makes bile.
9. Part of the body that churns and mixes food.
10. Part of the body that pumps blood through the blood vessels.

a. blood vessels
b. brain
c. heart
d. larynx
e. liver
f. lungs
g. muscles
h. oxygen
i. saliva
j. stomach

Number of Answers   10
Number Right   _____

Part 3: What Is the Healthful
        Thing to Do?

On a piece of paper copy the sentences below that tell healthful things to do. Do not copy sentences that are about unhealthful things to do.

1. Eat a good breakfast before you go to school.
2. Wash your hands before you eat.
3. Hurry off to school without any breakfast.
4. Wash your hands after you use the toilet.
5. Be sure to tell the teacher if you do not feel well at school.
6. Try not to miss school even if you have a bad cold.
7. Wash raw fruits and vegetables before you eat them.
8. Sit as close to the television set as you can.
9. Be sure to cover your nose and mouth when you cough or sneeze.
10. When you can, brush your teeth after you eat.
11. If you are sick at school, do not tell anyone.
12. Go to bed in time to get about eleven hours of sleep at night.

Health Books to Read

Here are some interesting books about health that you may find at the library.

About the Body, Its Care, and Safety

Fenton, Carroll L., and Turner, Eloise F. *Inside You and Me* (John Day).

Hinshaw, Alice. *The True Book of Your Body and You* (Childrens Press).

Leaf, Munro. *Safety Can Be Fun* (Lippincott).

Phleger, Frederick and Marjorie. *You Will Live Under the Sea* (Random).

Pounds, Elenore T., and Richmond, Julius B., M.D. *Drugs and Your Safety* (Scott, Foresman).

Ravielli, Anthony. *Wonders of the Human Body* (Viking).

Showers, Paul. *A Drop of Blood* (Crowell).

———. *Hear Your Heart* (Crowell).

———. *How Many Teeth?* (Crowell).

———. *Your Skin and Mine* (Crowell).

Smaridge, Norah. *Watch Out!* (Abingdon).

Zim, Herbert S. *Bones* (Morrow).

Exercise and Play

Borten, Helen. *Do You Move As I Do?* (Abelard-Schuman).

Fraser, Kathleen. *Stilts, Somersaults, and Headstands* (Atheneum).

Pounds, Elenore T., and Tillotson, Joan S. *Moving, Moving, Moving About* (Scott, Foresman).

Sanders, Lisbeth P. *Fit for Fun* (AMA).

Spier, Peter. *London Bridge Is Falling Down* (Doubleday).

Foods

Frisch, Rose E. *Plants That Feed the World* (Van Nostrand).

Paul, Aileen, and Hawkins, Arthur. *Kids Cooking* (Doubleday).

Scheib, Ida. *The First Book of Food* (Watts).

Solot, Mary Lynn. *100 Hamburgers: The Getting Thin Book* (Lothrop).

Van der Linde, Polly and Tasha. *Around the World in Eighty Dishes* (Scroll Press).

Microbes

Frahm, Anne. *The True Book of Bacteria* (Childrens Press).

Lewis, Lucia Z. *The First Book of Microbes* (Watts).

Lietz, Gerald S. *Junior Science Book of Bacteria* (Garrard).

Selsam, Millicent E. *Greg's Microscope* (Harper).

Environmental Education and Community Health

Kay, Eleanor. *Let's Find Out About Hospitals* (Watts).

Perera, Thomas B., and Orlowsky, Wallace. *Who Will Clean the Air?* (Coward).

Pounds, Elenore T., and others. A Health and Growth Enrichment Booklet series on environmental education: *Noise, Noise, Noise; Once There Was a River: A Story of Water Pollution; Wastebasket Full, Wastebasket Empty; Who Cares About Air Pollution?* (Scott, Foresman).

Radlauer, Edward and Ruth S. *Water for Your Community* (Childrens Press).

Schneider, Herman and Nina. *Let's Look Under the City* (Young Scott).

Growing Up

Desbarats, Peter. *Gabrielle and Selena* (Harcourt).

Estes, Eleanor. *The Moffats* (Harcourt).

Kuskin, Karla. *Any Me I Want to Be* (Harper).

Lexau, Joan M. *Benjie* (Dial).

Nordstrom, Ursula. *The Secret Language* (Harper).

Selsam, Millicent E. *All About Eggs and How They Change into Animals* (Young Scott).

Uhl, Melvin. *About Eggs and Creatures That Hatch from Them* (Childrens Press).

Van Stockum, Hilda. *Mogo's Flute* (Viking).

Warburg, Sandol Stoddard. *Growing Time* (Houghton).

Glossary

Full Pronunciation Key

The pronunciation of each word is shown just after the word, in this way: **ab bre vi ate** (ə brē′vē āt). The letters and signs used are pronounced as in the words at the right. The mark ′ is placed after a syllable with primary or heavy accent, as in the example above. The mark ′ after a syllable shows a secondary or lighter accent, as in **ab bre vi a tion** (ə brē′vē ā′shən).

Foreign Sound: н as in German ach. Pronounce k without closing the breath passage.

a	hat, cap		o	hot, rock
ā	age, face		ō	open, go
ä	father, far		ô	order, all
			oi	oil, voice
b	bad, rob		ou	house, out
ch	child, much			
d	did, red		p	paper, cup
			r	run, try
e	let, best		s	say, yes
ē	equal, be		sh	she, rush
ėr	term, learn		t	tell, it
			th	thin, both
f	fat, if		ŦH	then, smooth
g	go, bag			
h	he, how		u	cup, butter
			ù	full, put
i	it, pin		ü	rule, move
ī	ice, five			
			v	very, save
j	jam, enjoy		w	will, woman
k	kind, seek		y	young, yet
l	land, coal		z	zero, breeze
m	me, am		zh	measure, seizure
n	no, in			
ng	long, bring		ə	represents:

ə represents:
a in about
e in taken
i in April
o in lemon
u in circus

ər represents:
er in mother
ur in pursuit

This pronunciation key is from *Thorndike-Barnhart Beginning Dictionary* (Scott, Foresman and Company).

ac ci dent (ak′sə dənt), an event not wanted, intended, or planned to happen, such as the dropping of a dish, a fall from tripping over something in the dark, or the colliding of two automobiles.

an ti bi ot ic (an′ti bī ot′ik), chemical product of bacteria, yeast, and molds that destroys or weakens harmful microbes. *Penicillin is an antibiotic.*

back bone (bak′bōn′), the main bone along the middle of the back. It consists of many separate bones held together by ligaments, muscles, and tendons. The backbone is also called the *spine*.

bac ter i a (bak tir′ē ə), tiny living plants that can be seen only through a microscope. Some bacteria cause disease; others cause milk to sour or turn cider into vinegar.

bi cus pid (bī kus′pid), tooth having two cusps, or pointed ends, that tears and grinds food. An adult has eight bicuspids.

bile (bīl), a bitter, greenish liquid made by the liver that aids digestion of food; also called *gall*.

blood (blud), the red liquid in the blood vessels; the red liquid that flows from a cut. Blood is circulated by the heart, carries oxygen and digested food to all parts of the body, and takes away waste materials.

blood ves sels (blud′ ves′əlz), tubes in the body through which the blood circulates.

bone (bōn), the hard tissue forming the framework of the body.

bow el (bou′əl), the tube in the body into which food passes from the stomach; one of the divisions of the intestine.

brain (brān), a soft, spongy mass of nerve cells within the skull, or bony framework of the head.

breathe (brēTH), draw air into the lungs and force it out.

car bon di ox ide (kär′bən dī ok′sīd), a colorless, odorless gas, present in air. It is a waste product formed by the body and is removed from the body through breathing out.

cav i ty (kav′ə tē), *pl.* **cav i ties,** a hole in a tooth; a hollow place. Sticky, sweet foods left on the teeth cause cavities.

cell (sel), very small unit of living matter. All animals and plants are made of cells. There are blood cells, bone cells, muscle cells, nerve cells, and so on, in the human body.

cer e al (sir′ē əl), grain which is used as a food. Wheat, rice, and corn are cereals.

chem i cal (kem′ ə kəl), any simple substance (element) used to cause changes in other substances. Sulfuric acid, bicarbonate of soda, and borax are chemicals.

con tract (kən trakt′), draw together; make or become narrow; shorten; make or become smaller; shrink: *Muscles contract to help move bones.*

crown (kroun), part of a tooth which appears beyond the gum, or an artificial substitute for it.

cus pid (kus′ pid), tooth having one cusp, or pointed end, and used especially for tearing food. An adult has four cuspids.

den tal car ies (den′tl ker′ēz *or* kar′ēz), destruction of dental tissues; tooth decay.

den tist (den′tist), doctor who takes care of teeth. A dentist fills cavities in teeth, cleans them, moves them into place, extracts them, and supplies artificial teeth.

di gest (də jest′ *or* dī jest′), change food in the mouth, stomach, and intestines so that the body can use it: *We digest our food. The food is digested.*

di ges tion (də jes′chən), the changing or breaking down of food in the mouth, stomach, and intestines so that the body can use it.

dis ease (də zēz′), 1. sickness; illness. 2. any particular illness: *Measles and chicken pox are two diseases of children.*

dis ease germ (də zēz′ jėrm′), microbe that causes disease.

dis solve (di zolv′), make or become liquid, especially by putting or being put into a liquid: *Salt or sugar will dissolve in water.*

doc tor (dok′tər), person who treats diseases. A doctor is also called a *physician.*

ear (ir), the part of the body with which we hear.

e lec tron mi cro scope (i lek′tron mī′krə skōp), microscope that uses beams of electrons rather than beams of light to enlarge images, and that has much higher power than an ordinary light microscope.

e mo tions (i mō′shənz), *see* **feelings.**

ex er cise (ek′sər sīz), 1. practice; active use: *Exercise is good for the body and mind.* 2. give exercise to; train.

eye (ī), the part of the body with which we see.

feel ings (fē′lingz), ways of responding. We have feelings of joy, jealousy, shyness, hate, love, rage, excitement, and so on.

fill ing (fil′ing), substance placed in a space to fill it. A dentist puts a filling in a decayed tooth.

fil ter (fil′tər), device used for straining out substances from a liquid or gas by putting it slowly through felt, paper, sand, charcoal, and so on.

fil tra tion (fil trā′shən), process of passing a liquid or gas through a filter.

flu o ride (flü′ə rīd′), fluorine compound that may be added to drinking water in small amounts or applied by a dentist directly to the teeth to prevent tooth decay.

food (füd), what an animal or plant takes in to enable it to live and grow.

gall (gôl), *see* **bile.**

gall blad der (gôl′ blad′ər), the sac attached to the liver in which gall, or bile, from the liver is stored until needed for digestion.

gar bage (gär′bij), waste animal or vegetable matter from a home, store, industry, and so on.

germ (jėrm), a very tiny animal, plant, or other living organism which is too small to be seen without a microscope; a microbe. The microbes that cause disease are called germs: *the germs of pneumonia.*

gill (gil), part of the body of a fish, tadpole, crab, and so on, arranged for breathing in water.

gland (gland), organ in the body which makes and gives out some substance which helps the body do its work. The liver and the pancreas are glands.

growth (grōth), process of growing; development.

gum (gum), flesh around the teeth.

hatch (hach), 1. bring forth (young) from an egg or eggs. 2. to emerge from an egg: *A chicken hatches from an egg.*

health (helth), 1. being well or not sick; freedom from illness of any kind. 2. condition of the body: *good health, poor health.*

heart (härt), the organ that pumps blood throughout the body.

im mu ni ty (i myü′nə tē), *pl.* **im mu ni ties,** one's protection against or resistance to communicable disease.

im pu ri ty (im pyür′ə tē), *pl.* **im pu ri ties,** 1. something that is dirty, filthy, or unclean. 2. thing that makes something else impure: *Filtering the water removed some of its impurities.*

in cin er a tor (in sin′ə rā′tər), furnace or other arrangement for burning things.

in ci sor (in sī′zər), tooth having a sharp edge for cutting; one of the front teeth. There are eight incisors in the permanent set of teeth.

in fect (in fekt′), cause disease in by introducing germs: *Dirt infects an open cut.*

jaw bone (jô′bōn′), bone of either jaw, especially the bone of the lower jaw.

joint (joint), in animals and humans, a place where two bones move on each other.

kid ney (kid′nē), one of the pair of organs in mammals, birds, and reptiles that take waste matter and excess water from the blood and pass them off through the bladder.

lab o ra to ry (lab′rə tôr′ē), *pl.* **lab o ra to ries,** place where scientific work is done: *a chemical laboratory.*

large in tes tine (lärj′ in tes′tən), the tube which receives the undigested food from the small intestine and passes it out of the body.

lar yn gi tis (lar ən jī′tis), inflammation of the larynx. A person with laryngitis has a very sore throat and can hardly talk.

lar ynx (lar′ingks), the organ at the upper end of the windpipe where voice is produced. The larynx is also called the *voice box.*

liv er (liv′ər), the large, reddish-brown gland that makes bile, aids in the absorption of food, and stores food until it is needed by the body. The liver is the body's largest gland.

lo co mo tor move ment (lō′kə mō′tər müv′mənt), an action in which the body moves from place to place, as in walking, skipping, hopping, and so on.

lung (lung), one of the pair of breathing organs found in the chest. By means of the lungs the blood receives oxygen.

mem brane (mem′brān), a thin, flexible layer of tissue or other living material which lines or covers cells, organs, and other parts of the body.

---

hat, āge, fär;   let, bē, tėrm;   it, īce;   hot, gō, ôrder;   oil, out;   cup, pu̇t, rüle;   takən, mothər

men tal health (men′tl helth′). A person has good mental health when he can manage upset feelings in ways that help him but do not hurt others.

mi crobe (mī′krōb), *see* **microörganism.**

mi cro ör gan ism (mī′krō ôr′gə niz′əm), animal or plant organism too small to be seen except with a microscope. Germs are microörganisms.

mi cro scope (mī′krə skōp), an instrument for making enlarged images of small objects invisible or not clearly visible to the naked eye.

mo lar (mō′lər), a tooth with a broad surface for grinding. A person's back teeth are molars.

mold (mōld), a microörganism of the plant kingdom which appears as a woolly or furry growth on food and other surfaces and is often black or greenish in color.

mo tor nerve (mō′tər nėrv′), bundle of nerve fibers that arouse muscles to action. When you want to walk or talk, motor nerves carry messages from the brain or spinal cord to the muscles.

mus cle (mus′əl), tissue of the body that is capable of contracting, or shortening, and relaxing to help the body move.

nerve (nėrv), a fiber or bundle of fibers connecting the brain or spinal cord with the eyes, ears, muscles, glands, and so on.

non lo co mo tor move ment (non′lō kə mō′tər müv′mənt), a movement made while the body stays in one place.

nu cle us (nü′klē əs *or* nyü′klē əs), an active body lying within the protoplasm of a cell of an animal or a plant, without which the cell cannot divide and grow.

nurse (nėrs), person who takes care of the sick or the old, or is trained to do this.

or gan (ôr′gən), any part of the body that has a special job to do to help the body perform as it should. The eyes, stomach, heart, and lungs are organs of the body.

ox y gen (ok′sə jən), a gas without color or odor that is present in the air. It is taken into the body by breathing.

pan cre as (pan′krē əs), a gland near the stomach that pours into the small intestine a substance that helps digestion.

pas teur ize (pas′chə rīz′ *or* pas′tə rīz′), heat (milk, and so on) hot enough and long enough to kill certain germs.

pen i cil lin (pen′ə sil′ ən), a very useful antibiotic drug made by a mold.

per ma nent teeth (pėr′mə nənt tēth′), the second set of teeth (32), which come in when the primary teeth are shed. The permanent teeth are intended to last a lifetime.

plaque (plak), sticky, colorless film of harmful germs which is always forming on the teeth.

pol lute (pə lüt′), make dirty: *The water at the beach was polluted by waste from the factory.*

pol lu tion (pə lü′shən), lack of purity; uncleanness: *air pollution, water pollution.*

pos ture (pos′chər), the position of the body; way of holding the body.

pri ma ry teeth (prī′mer ē *or* prī′mə rē tēth), the first set of teeth (20), which are later replaced by the permanent set of teeth.

pro to plasm (prō′tə plaz′əm), living matter; the colorless, jellylike, living substance of which all plant and animal cells are made.

quar ry (kwôr′ē), *pl.* **quar ries,** place where stone is dug, cut, or blasted out, usually for building purposes.

rec tum (rek′təm), the lowest part of the large intestine, where undigested food is held until it is passed out of the body.

red blood cells (red′ blud′ selz′), cells that with the white blood cells form a large part of the blood. Red blood cells contain hemoglobin, which gives them their color. Red blood cells carry oxygen from the lungs to various parts of the body.

re lax (rē laks′), to loosen up; to make less tense: *Relax your muscles to rest them.*

rib (rib), one of the curved bones extending round the chest from the backbone to the front of the body.

root (rüt), the part of a tooth that is covered by the gums and cannot be seen.

safe ty (sāf′tē), 1. freedom from harm or danger: *You can cross the street in safety when the policeman holds up his hand.* 2. bringing no harm or danger; preventing harm: *a safety belt.*

sa li va (sə lī′və), the liquid that the salivary glands pour into the mouth to keep it moist, aid in chewing, and start digestion.

san i tar i an (san′ə ter′ē ən), a specialist in sanitary science and public health (milk, food, and so on).

san i tar y (san′ə ter′ē), 1. of or having to do with health; favorable to health; preventing disease. 2. free from dirt and filth.

sense (sens), power of the mind to know what happens outside itself. Sight, smell, taste, hearing, and touch are the five main senses: *A dog has a keen sense of hearing.*

sen sor y nerve (sen′sər ē nėrv′), bundle of nerve fibers that carry messages from the sense organs to the brain. Pain, temperature, touch, sight, smell, sound, and taste are conveyed by sensory nerves.

sew age (sü′ij), waste matter which passes through sewers.

shot (shot), dose of a drug in the form of an injection, given to make the body able to resist a particular communicable disease.

six-year mo lar (siks′yir′ mō′lər), one of the first permanent teeth to come in. There are four of them, and they appear at about six years of age.

skel e ton (skel′ə tən), the bones of a body fitted together in their natural places. The skeleton is a frame that supports the muscles, organs, and so on.

skin (skin), the covering of the body.

skull (skul), bony framework of the head and face.

---

hat, āge, fär; let, bē, tėrm; it, īce; hot, gō, ôrder; oil, out; cup, pùt, rüle; takən, mothər

sludge (sluj), soft, thick, muddy deposit.

small in tes tine (smôl′ in tes′tən), the long, winding tube which receives partly digested food from the stomach. The small intestine completes the digestion of food.

space main tain er (spās′ mān tā′nər), a temporary appliance inserted in place of a missing tooth to keep the teeth next to it from moving out of place.

spine (spīn), *see* **backbone.**

spore (spôr), a microscopic part of a plant which can resist heat, cold, and dryness and can grow into a new plant. Ferns, bacteria, and molds produce spores.

spright ly (sprīt′lē), lively; spirited.

state ly (stāt′lē), dignified; imposing; grand; majestic: *The Capitol at Washington is a stately building.*

steth o scope (steth′ə skōp), instrument used by doctors to listen to sounds in the heart and lungs.

stom ach (stum′ək), a large, muscular bag which mixes the food and digests some of it before passing it on into the small intestine.

tem per a ture (tem′pər ə chər), degree of heat or cold. The temperature of freezing water is 32° F. The normal temperature of a person is approximately 98.6° F.

throat (thrōt), 1. the front of the neck. 2. the passage at the back of the mouth leading to the stomach and to the lungs.

tis sue (tish′ü), a mass of similar cells which performs a particular function: *brain tissue.*

tongue (tung), the movable piece of flesh in the mouth. The tongue is used for tasting, in chewing, and, by people, in talking.

ton sil (ton′səl), either of the two small oval masses on the sides of the throat, just back of the mouth.

tooth (tüth), one of the hard bonelike parts in the mouth, used for biting and chewing.

trunk (trungk), 1. the main part of anything: *the trunk of a column.* 2. a body without the head, arms, and legs.

un safe (un sāf′), dangerous.

u ri nar y blad der (yùr′ə ner′e blad′ər), a soft thin, muscular bag in the body that receives and stores urine from the kidneys.

u rine (yùr′ən), the fluid made up of wastes and water taken out of the blood by the kidneys.

vi rus (vī′rəs), any of a group of disease-producing microörganisms that reproduce only inside living cells and are too small to be seen through an ordinary microscope.

voice box (vois′ boks′), *see* **larynx.**

waste (wāst), 1. make poor use of; throw away. 2. waste material; stuff that is left over.

white blood cells (whīt′ blud′ selz′), cells that float in the blood and lymph. Some of them destroy disease germs.

---

hat, āge, fär;   let, bē, tėrm;   it, īce;   hot, gō, ôrder;   oil, out;   cup, pùt, rüle;   takən, mothər

Index

Index of Health and Safety Ideas[1]

---

[1]Selected behavioral objectives for this level are given in the
Resource Book, page 27.

About the Book

A Health Program for Eight- to Nine-Year-Olds

Book Three of the HEALTH AND GROWTH Program[1] has been designed especially to meet the health and safety needs, interests, and curiosities of children who are eight years old or thereabouts.

Youngsters this age have a lively curiosity about their bodies and what's inside them. Appetites are improving, and this is a golden age for encouraging children to try out new foods and to investigate new ways of serving foods.

Boys and girls this age tend to be energetic and to show enthusiasm for strenuous activities. They relish a chance to explore the wide range of movements their bodies can make.

Differences in growth patterns are becoming ever more apparent, and children need to learn that each individual has his or her own timetable for growing. Like all human beings, these eight- to nine-year-olds profit from opportunities to consider how to cope with upset feelings.

The safety needs of this venturesome age group include guidance in the areas of bicycle, fire, water, and playground safety, and in the development of wholesome attitudes toward accident prevention.

Pupils are given an overview, too, of how community health workers and a concern for environmental health can all contribute to our well-being. A unique feature of *Book Three* is the photographic essays of the work of a public health nurse and of other community health workers.

To facilitate effective teaching, the material is presented in short units. Each unit, in turn, includes enriching activities and simple tests. Additional teaching suggestions appear throughout the annotated *Teacher's Edition,* which includes a special *Resource Book.*

Readability

Book Three utilizes, for the most part, words that are common to the third-grade reading level. Readability checks and classroom tryouts of the material in prepublication form indicate that the text is suitable for use in Grade Three.

---

[1]The HEALTH AND GROWTH Program includes *Off to a Good Start* (Junior Primer Activity Sheets), and *Book One* through *Book Eight* with accompanying *Teachers' Editions.* Also available is a preprimary health program, *Health and Safety Highlights: Pictures and Songs for Young Children.*

Credits

Cover: Photograph by Ralph Cowan.
Unit 1: 9—Photograph by Lyle Mayer. 10-25—Anatomical art by Lou Barlow. 26—Photograph by Lyle Mayer. 30-33—Anatomical art by Lou Barlow. 34, 35—Photographs by James Ballard. 37—Photographs by R. Stuart Weeks, M.D., Department of Otolaryngology, The University of Chicago, Chicago, Illinois. 38, 39—Anatomical art by Lou Barlow. 40, 41—Drawings by George Suyeoka.
Unit 2: 45, 47, 49, 51, 53, 55, 57, 59, 61, 63, 65, 67—Photographs by Michel Ditlove. 50, 58, 60—Drawings by Mel Klapholz. 70—Drawings by George Suyeoka.
Unit 3: 75, 77-80—Anatomical art by Lou Barlow. 82-83—Photograph by Lyle Mayer. 84, 85—Photographs by Norman H. Olsen, D.D.S. 86, 87—Anatomical art by Lou Barlow. 89—Drawing by George Suyeoka.
Unit 4: 92-97—Photographs by Myles DeRussy. 94-97—Anatomical art by Lou Barlow. 98-109—Photographs by Myles DeRussy. 111, 113—Drawings by George Suyeoka.
Unit 5: 116-125—Photographs by Ralph Cowan. 126-129, 131—Drawings by George Suyeoka.
Unit 6: 134—Photograph by Rhodes Patterson, 136—Photograph by James Ballard. 137 (Top Left, Top Right)—Photographs courtesy of Clay Adams, Division of Becton, Dickinson and Company, Parsippany, New Jersey. 137 (Bottom), 138, 139—Courtesy Dr. Leon J. LeBeau, Department of Microbiology, University of Illinois at the Medical Center, Chicago, Illinois. 140—Photograph by James Ballard. 141 (Top Left)—Courtesy of the American Society for Microbiology. 141 (Top Right)—Courtesy of the Virus Laboratory, University of California, Berkeley, California. 141 (Bottom)—Courtesy A. R. Taylor, Ph.D., Laboratory Director–Virus Research, Parke, Davis & Co. 142 (Top Left, Top Right)—Photographs by James Ballard. 142 (Bottom)—Photograph courtesy of Clay Adams, Division of Becton, Dickinson and Company, Parsippany, New Jersey. 143 (Top Left, Top Right)—Courtesy Dr. Leon J. LeBeau, Department of Microbiology, University of Illinois at the Medical Center, Chicago, Illinois. 143 (Bottom)—Courtesy Charles Pfizer & Company, Inc. 145—Courtesy Dr. James G. Hirsch, The Rockefeller University. 146, 147—Photographs by Myles DeRussy. 149-151—Drawings by George Suyeoka.
Unit 7: 154-161—Photographs by Archie Lieberman. 162, 163—Photographs courtesy of Department of Streets and Sanitation, City of Chicago. 164-171—Photographs by Archie Lieberman. 173—Drawings by George Suyeoka. Grateful acknowledgment is also extended to these departments of the City of Chicago for allowing us to photograph situations pictured in Unit 7: Board of Health, Department of Air Pollution Control, Department of Streets and Sanitation, Department of Water and Sewers.
Unit 8: 176—Photograph by James Ballard. 178, 179—Photographs by Myles DeRussy. 180-183—Drawings by Mel Klapholz. 185, 188, 189—Photographs by Myles DeRussy. 192, 195—Drawings by George Suyeoka.
Grateful acknowledgment is made to the following companies whose products appear on page 119: Certified Grocers of Illinois, Inc., for Raggedy Ann; Del Monte Corporation; General Foods Corporation for Bird's Eye; and the Green Giant and the Giant Figure, trademarks of and used with the permission of Green Giant Company. For permission to reproduce the cover of their book on page 172: Franklin Watts, Inc., for *First Book of Nursing* by Mary Elting © 1951.
For coöperation in photographing situations on pages 51, 61, 63—The Laboratory School, Evanston, Illinois; on pages 158, 159—Leon's Sausage Company and Hawthorn-Mellody Farms Dairy.